J.M. + J.

Salve, Regina, Decor Carmeli,

SAINTS WESTWARD

Saints Westward

Some Colorful and Heroic Men
and Women Who Planted and
Watered the Seed of the Faith
in the Western Hemisphere

BY

DONALD ATTWATER

WITH DRAWINGS BY

Sister Mary of the Compassion, O.P.

New York

P. J. KENEDY & SONS

NIHIL OBSTAT: RT. REV. MSGR. JOHN M. A. FEARNS, S.T.D., *Censor Librorum*

IMPRIMATUR: ✠ FRANCIS CARDINAL SPELLMAN, *Archbishop of New York*

New York, February 24, 1953

The *nihil obstat* and imprimatur are official declarations that a book or pamphlet is free of doctrinal and moral error. No implication is contained therein that those who have granted the *nihil obstat* and *imprimatur* agree with the contents, opinions or statements expressed.

In conformity with the decree of Pope Urban VIII, we do not wish to anticipate the judgment of the Church in our appraisal of the characters and occurrences spoken of herein. We submit wholeheartedly to the infallible wisdom and judgment of Holy Mother Church.

A portion of this book appeared in *St. Joseph Magazine,* Copyright 1952, 1953, by *St. Joseph Magazine.*

*TO ALL
MY AMERICAN
FRIENDS*

PREFACE

ꝏ

MOST of these sketches appeared in the *St. Joseph Magazine* and I must thank the editor, Dom Albert Bauman, and the proprietors, the Benedictine monks of Mount Angel, Oregon, first for giving them hospitality, and then for allowing them to be reprinted.

A series devoted to the holy ones of the American continent is naturally concerned in the first place with those who have been actually canonized or beatified. But it need not be restricted to them: it should include at least some of those servants of God whose cause has been begun, or which may be undertaken in the future. I have therefore, in addition to noticing all the saints and beati of North and South America, included six others. The causes of the beatification of four of them, Kateri Tekakwitha, Mary Martin, Father Serra, and Mother Seton, have been begun and are in various stages of progress. Gregory Lopez is included because of his interest, and because he has for long had what is called a "popular *cultus*" and is commonly referred to as Blessed. And I chose the less-known Samuel Mazzuchelli to represent all the rest. I think nothing further by way of introduction to a small book is necessary—except a word of apology that I, an Englishman, should venture to offer to the American public a book about some of its own people.   D. A.

CONTENTS

SAINTS WESTWARD

Sing ye to the Lord a new song, his praise is from the ends of the earth; you that go down to the sea, and all that are therein; ye islands and ye inhabitants of them. *Isa. 42:10*

1

THE SAINTS AND US

W HO was the first saint who was a citizen of the United
States? Nobody knows. Nobody ever will know in this
world. It is a question that only God can answer.

"But," I hear somebody say, "I thought that St. Frances
Cabrini was the first canonized saint of the United States."
Yes, she is. *Canonized* saint. But there are other saints. Many
famous saints have never been canonized, strictly speaking;
many more have not only not been canonized, but they are
not even known. When Blessed Philippine Duchesne died in
1852, Father de Smet wrote of her, "No greater saint ever
died in Missouri, or perhaps in the whole Union." Of course
Father de Smet was speaking rhetorically, as we say; he knew
there must have been saints in Missouri and the Union, but
he could not be sure that Blessed Philippine was the greatest,
because neither he nor anyone else knew who the others were.
And anyway it is not easy for any human being to decide which
saint is greater and which not so great. But the point is this,
that there had already been saints in the Union, uncanonized
and unknown.

I am afraid we often forget these unknown saints. (We may
have one living next door to us right now.) But the Church
does not forget, and she does not mean us to forget either. For

3

every year on November 1 she celebrates most solemnly the
feast of All Saints: not only the famous and the canonized,
but *all* saints (known to man or known only to God) who in
whatever circumstances and whatever states of life have
"fought the good fight," and now enjoy the happiness of God
for ever in Heaven. "Let us rejoice in the Lord," we sing,
"as we keep holiday in honor of all the saints" . . . "a great
multitude, past all counting, taken from all nations and tribes
and peoples and languages."

If a man or a woman is a saint, then he or she is a saint
whether anybody knows it or not. *Canonized* saints are not
only known; they are publicly recognized and declared by the
Church to have been heroically good during their lives on
earth and to be now with God in Heaven.

The Church was already 900 years old before a pope, John
XV, made the first public declaration of somebody's sanctity
to the whole world; and it was longer still before there was
the fixed process of canonization, preceded by beatification,
that we have today. Before those times people were canonized
in various ways: the apostles and other early holy ones by
universal consent, the early martyrs by veneration at the place
of their martyrdom, and so on. Later on, bishops canonized
by giving permission for a feast to be kept in somebody's
honor; and the veneration of a saint in one diocese would
spread to another, and perhaps to the whole Church. Many
of the greatest saints—St. Martin, St. Basil, St. Benedict, St.
Augustine, for example—were canonized in this or a similar
way.

It is a mistake to suppose that there is anywhere a complete
and official list even of saints who have been canonized in one

way or another. We hear references to "the Church's calendar"; but there is not one completely uniform calendar used throughout the Church—it varies considerably in different places and religious orders. The official general calendar that we Catholics of the Latin rite find printed in our missals and prayerbooks includes the feast days of only some 300 saints, including, of course, most of the greatest. The Roman Martyrology (from which a passage is read aloud every day in monasteries) contains about 5,000 names, which include many others besides martyrs. The Dominican calendar has about 70 saints and *beati* not appearing elsewhere, the Syrian calendar about 100, and so on. In all the other calendars and martyrologies, still in use or used in the past, there are thousands more names.

The late Monsignor F. G. Holweck, of Saint Louis, in his *Biographical Dictionary of the Saints* tried to include all the known saints and blessed. There are at least 15,000 names in that volume, perhaps nearer 20,000. Of many of them little or nothing is known except their names and countries and approximate dates; and only a small proportion were canonized by our modern papal process. But they were all honored by those who have gone before us in various parts of the world.

And then there are all the unnumbered, unknown saints, men and women. How true it is, according to St. Paul, that we have "a great cloud of witnesses" over our heads, "who have gone before us with the sign of faith," says the prayer for the dead at Mass.

An American priest once told me how impressed he was in his travels about Europe by the evidences everywhere of the saints: the very ground, trodden by them, seemed to be holy. And it is quite true that in Europe and the nearer parts of Asia one is continually reminded of holy men and women: their memories and influence are everywhere with us, in spite of the weight of our sins and follies which throughout the ages have been monstrous. That sort of consciousness of the saints is a privilege which in your own country you Americans do not have—shall I say, do not have *yet*. You share with us the prayers and memories and veneration of the saints of the Old World; you can make them your spiritual companions and examples just as we can. But you do not have the help and inspiration of, so to speak, meeting them every day in the places where they lived.

On the banks of the Mississippi is the city of Saint Louis, named for a great French saint. But Louis the saint had nothing to do with Saint Louis the city, which did not come into existence till 500 years after the saint's death. Whereas I at this moment am writing in the little town of Saint Ives, near the southwest tip of England, named for St. Ia, who centuries ago lived at this corner of the coast. I look out of my window and I see the sea and rocky headlands as she saw them, and the very spot perhaps where she built her hermitage.

It is fine that in America there should be cities and townships called Saint Augustine, Saint Joseph, Saint Paul, Saint John's, and the like. But Saint Albans in England, Strath-*fillan* in Scotland, Llani*lltyd* in Wales, Down*patrick* in Ireland, Saint-Denis in France, Saint-Gall in Switzerland, San Marino in Italy, the *Ruperts*berg in Germany, and dozens more—all derive their name from a saint who actually lived or died there. Often, as at Saint Albans, the very existence of the place today is due to the saint's shrine there in the past. But names are a small part of it. Throughout Europe and beyond we walk and talk, rejoice and grieve, in the very places where the saints walked and talked, rejoiced and grieved before us: from St. Columba at Iona, an island off the west coast of Scotland, to St. Ephraem beyond the Euphrates River in Iraq; from St. Ignatius Loyola at Manresa in Spain to St. Sergius in his monastery near Moscow; from St. Augustine in North Africa to St. Anskar in Scandinavia.

We Europeans, of course, venerate all the well-known saints of the Church equally with you Americans: from our Lady, St. Peter and St. Paul and the rest of the apostles, who of course have a special place of dignity before all others, to St. Anthony of Padua and St. Thérèse of Lisieux; wherever you find people of Irish origin you find St. Patrick, and where there are Catholics, there is St. Joseph.

But perhaps many American Catholics do not realize how living is the devotion to *local* saints in the various parts of Europe. It is sometimes said that Catholics in England do not have enough devotion to their own saints. I am afraid there is truth in that. But the fact remains that the Church in Great Britain observes the feasts of nearly 100 English, Welsh, and Scottish saints who do not appear in the general calendar—and that is without counting our beatified martyrs of the Reformation. Or look at Ireland: 50 and more Irish saints are celebrated in her churches every year, whose names are mostly unknown elsewhere. In some countries of the continent, France, for example, the proportion of local saints must be very high.

To be able to look upon the actual buildings or scenes that

the saints themselves saw makes them wonderfully real and "living." That must be especially so in such districts as north-western Italy, where there have been so many canonized saints and blessed living within the last 100 years. But—if I may again refer to my own country, which after all is the one I know best—it is also true of the English Reformation martyrs of 300 and 400 years ago. In spite of all the changes since then, when we read their lives we recognize the sort of people we know, moving in places that, however altered, are familiar to us, sometimes with details that are still true today.

You see that old house standing alone in the main square at Hereford? Blessed John Kemble's eyes must have rested on that as he was taken to martyrdom, after smoking a last pipe of tobacco with the sheriff. . . . Another old house in another city, York. It was once the home of a young woman, the mother of children, who was crushed to death with weights near by because she refused to plead to the "crime" of sheltering hunted priests. She was Blessed Margaret Clitherow. . . . Blessed David Lewis was a Jesuit who was betrayed and brought to death by an apostate woman who had declared, "I'll wash my hands in Mr. Lewis's blood, and make a stew of his head!" We can, as it were, follow the hoof tracks of his horse in the Monmouthshire lanes, and visit lonely houses where he celebrated Mass in secret. When the martyrs under the Chinese Boxers were beatified in 1946, there were present in St. Peter's a granddaughter of one of the martyrs, and also a Chinese nun who had witnessed the martyrdoms, had been tortured herself, and had had the blood of a martyr forced down her throat. . . . We all know that her mother was present at the canonization of St. Mary Goretti in 1950. . . . And here in England we can meet people who tell us, proudly and humbly: "I am a descendant of St. Thomas More." "And I of Blessed Adrian Fortescue." "And I of Blessed Margaret Pole," and others.

Certainly things of this sort make us realize that the saints of the past still live in a double way, actually in Heaven, but also in the hearts and minds of those who are enabled to remember and "picture" them vividly. It is indeed difficult to imagine St. Simeon Stylites on his pillar, or a Roman girl like St. Agnes, or Pope St. Gregory the Great chatting in the market place, and to grasp at once what they can mean for us. But St. Bernadette and St. Joseph Cafasso and St. Thomas More are to the French, the Italians, the English, one of themselves, flesh of their flesh, bone of their bone. And in this way the reality of the communion of saints becomes clearer and more full of meaning.

The time will come when Americans will have this joy and privilege. We are happy to see the beginning. Apart from the recognized saints of South America, whom perhaps we think of as Spanish rather than American, there are St. John de Brébeuf and the other North American martyrs, St. Frances Cabrini, Italian by birth but a United States citizen, Blessed Philippine Duchesne and Blessed Margaret Bourgeoys, both French by birth but living many years and dying, the one in the Middle West, the other in Canada.

All the above, except two of the martyrs, St. René Goupil and St. John Lalande, were priests or nuns. But it may well be that among the future canonized saints of North America will be many more lay men and women. I will even venture to say I think it is probable. It is sometimes pointed out that there are far more saints among monks and nuns than among lay people, far more among bishops than priests, far more among men than women. This is true numerically of those who are canonized or beatified. But nobody knows whether or not it be true of the *unknown* saints. From the very publicity of his position the saintliness of a bishop is more likely to become known than that of a priest in some obscure parish; a religious order is able to take an interest in and promote the cause of its holy members, but there is nobody to do that for lay people, unless the attention of the local bishop be called to them. It should be remembered that the public recognition of holiness by the Church is a process that usually begins at the bottom, so to speak, and progresses upward. The Holy See rarely moves in this matter until a bishop or bishops have asked her to do so; and in his turn a bishop rarely does anything about it until he knows that his people want him to.

In recent years a greater proportion of priests than bishops have been canonized or beatified, and a greater proportion of women, mostly foundresses of religious congregations. There have been more lay people too: St. Thomas More (it is agreed that he deserved canonization even if he had not been a martyr), St. Mary Goretti, Blessed Ann Mary Taigi, Blessed Contardo Ferrini, Blessed Dominic Savio. This is likely to go on. The Church holds up the ideal of holiness equally before everybody; the means of grace are the same for all, whether pope or housewife. To be a saint is very difficult; but it is no more difficult for a lay person, as such, than for a priest or a nun; it is impossible for either without the grace of God. The Church *wants* to canonize lay people. At the same time, it is possible to be *too* conscious of the distinctions between "cleric" and "lay." The Church consists of *all* her members. It is more important that we are Catholic Christians than that we are priests or lay people.

It is not my business to "preach"; but perhaps I shall not do wrong to put down here a thought that often comes to me. So many of us know so little about the actual lives the saints led; some of us don't know even the names of many of them, except for those who may be "popular" at the moment—St. Anthony of Padua, St. Thérèse of Lisieux, St. Jude.

But, taking those three as examples, the finding of things lost, the "shower of roses," the help in desperate cases, are not the most important things about them. All three are saints in Heaven simply because of their holy lives when on earth. As well, Anthony was a relentless and eloquent preacher against error and wickedness, a doctor—teacher—of the Church; Thérèse was an exemplary Carmelite nun; Jude was one of Jesus Christ's own personal apostles, a fellow worker with St. Peter. Those are the things that matter; without that holiness and those lives there would have been no "findings," no "roses," no help—at any rate from them. Yet I am afraid their popularity is due more to what we hope they will do for us than to appreciation of what they were themselves. We take the trouble to go to Mass on a first Friday, but perhaps not on the feast day of one of the Lord's apostles or other great saint.

There is a movie in which a schoolgirl, in a moment of exasperation, calls St. Ann a "snitcher." Two nuns overhear her. One protests: the other says, "But what faith! A girl must have great faith in a saint before she will call her a snitcher." I think that second nun was not necessarily right. It is possible for anyone who said that to have had, not a fine faith, but a "low" and ignorant idea, even a superstitious idea, about the saints in Heaven, what they can do and what is their relation to us and to Almighty God. It may be we sometimes too readily mistake for simple faith what is really simple and deplorable ignorance. St. Matthew in Chapter xx of his gospel tells us how the mother of the sons of Zebedee came to Jesus and asked for something she ought not to have asked for—doubtless in complete innocence and good faith. We are told our Lord's reply: "You know not what you ask," and He explained why. But we are not told that He commended her simple faith.

The Church wants us to ask the saints to intercede with Almighty God in behalf of our temporal needs. But the Church wants other things more. In the first place, she wants us to love and honor the saints—and the more we know about them the better we can do that. And then she wants us to look on them as examples, not as patterns to be mechanically copied, but as inspirations for our own living; and this we cannot do unless we know something about them.

In this matter, as in others, the Church shows us the way in her worship. "Pray for us, all you holy ones of God," she cries, "that we may be made worthy of the promises of Christ." Not made rich or successful or powerful or clever (though these things need not be despised), but *worthy*. Worthy of the promises of Christ—that those who love Him and try to follow Him shall not be overcome by temptation in this world, and shall live forever with Him and His saints in the next.

Spain, Cyprian, Perpetua, Felicity, and the martyrs of Uganda in Africa, Boniface in Germany and Holland, the martyrs of Lyons and of the Revolution in France, and many, many others in these and other countries.

But the first martyrs actually on the American continent were of course SS. John de Brébeuf and his companions in the north and BB. Roque Gonzalez and his companions in Paraguay. So well are they known, so much has been written about the North American martyrs, especially since their canonization in 1930, that it seems superfluous to tell the whole glorious story again. Let us then simply remind ourselves who these eight men were, and when and how they suffered; and in the first place that two of them were lay men, *donnés*—"oblates," if you like—who had given themselves to the service of the mission in which their five fellow martyrs were Jesuit priests.

The very first to give his life was one of these *donnés*, St. René Goupil. He had become a Jesuit novice in France, but had to leave the Society because of bad health. So he studied surgery, went to Canada to work in a hospital at Quebec, and joined St. Isaac Jogues on the Huron mission. Captured by the Iroquois, he was horribly tortured; and his face was so disfigured that Father Jogues applied to him the words of the prophet Isaias that are so often used of our Lord in his passion: "There is no beauty in him nor comeliness; we have seen him, and there was no sightliness that we should desire him." On September 29, 1642, at Ossernenon (Auriesville) in what is now upper New York State, Goupil was tomahawked for making the sign of the cross on an Indian child.

After a year of slavery and torments Father Jogues was

enabled to escape by the Protestant Dutch of Fort Orange. (He is the first priest known to have visited Manhattan Island.) But he was determined to preach the gospel to the Mohawks, and three years later he was back in Ossernenon, with the other *donné*, St. John Lalande. But the Bear clan looked on him as a sorcerer, and on October 18, 1646, he was treacherously slain, and Lalande met a like fate on the following day.

The Jesuit missionaries were making special efforts to convert the more promising Hurons, against whom the Iroquois were waging relentless hostilities. In 1648 a sudden attack was made on the Huron village of Teanaustaye, near Hillsdale in Ontario, just as St. Anthony Daniel had finished celebrating Mass. The people were panic-stricken, and so many implored baptism that Father Daniel had to sprinkle them with water from a streaming handkerchief. He would not try to escape, and the Iroquois shot him to death with arrows and threw his body into the burning chapel.

In the following year a raid was made on Saint-Louis, near Midland, Ontario, where St. John de Brébeuf and St. Gabriel Lalemant were stationed. At twenty-eight Brébeuf had been a tuberculous invalid in France, unable to make proper theological studies: he was now fifty-six, with sixteen years of tireless evangelization behind him and the reputation of being the best of all the missionaries among the Hurons. Lalemant had, years before in Paris, made a vow to sacrifice his life to the Indians. That vow was now to be redeemed, in terrible circumstances. The two priests were dragged away to Saint-Ignace, and the torments that they there endured are among the most horrible in the annals of martyrdom and the record of inhuman cruelty. Father Brébeuf continued to admonish his torturers and encourage their other Christian captives so long as he was capable of speech, and was silenced only when his lips were torn from his face. The Indians ate the roasted flesh of their victims, and drank their blood that they might thus be endowed with a like courage and fortitude. In that abomination may be seen an extraordinary caricature of one of the sublime truths that the martyrs died to teach them.[1]

Before the year 1649 was out, the other two martyrs had received their crowns. On December 7 there was a frightful massacre by Iroquois at the village of Saint-Jean of the Tobacco nation. St. Charles Garnier was shot down, and as he crawled to succor a dying Indian he was brained by a blow from a hatchet. The next day his companion, St. Noel Chabanel, returning from another village, was murdered by an apostate Huron. There is something especially moving about the fate of Garnier and Chabanel, for there was nothing in any sense "tough" about either of them: if St. John de Brébeuf was the "lion" of the mission, they were the "lambs." St. Noel in particular: he couldn't learn the languages of the Indians, he found them personally repellent—their habits, their food, everything about them, revolted him. What is more, throughout all his six years in Canada he was tried by spiritual dryness and lack of all warmth and consolation. So, lest he should be tempted to desert, he bound himself by a vow never to leave the Indian mission, where, being dead, he yet speaks to us.

[1] In the summer of 1952 members of the Indian-archaeology school of the University of Western Ontario discovered what is believed to be the site of SS. John and Gabriel's mission chapel at Saint-Louis.

But if the story of these martyrs is familiar to all of us, their three fellow Jesuits who met their death a score of years earlier in Paraguay are not nearly so well known in North America. These earliest martyrs of the Americas who have been raised to the altars of the Church suffered in 1628. They were not, of course, the first martyrs of the New World: three Franciscans were killed by Caribs in the Antilles in 1516; massacres on the mainland of South America soon followed; and in 1544 Friar Juan de Padilla was slain while at prayer, the first martyr of North America. Where he suffered is not certain—eastern Colorado, western Kansas, Texas have all been suggested. But these and others have not been beatified, for lack of sufficient certain evidence about the circumstances of their death. Such evidence may turn up some day.

Then, too, five years later, there were the Dominicans, Father Louis Cancer de Barbastro with his fellow friars, Father James Peñalosa and Brother Fuentes. They were murdered by Indians on the coast of Florida, yet their names are curiously little known, though Doctor John Gilmary Shea has written that Father Cancer was "one of the most remarkable missionaries of his order, whose wonderful sway over the Indians of Central America justified a confidence that the same means would influence the Mobilian tribes" of Florida.[2] Meanwhile the earliest beatified martyrs of America were three Jesuits of Paraguay, and one of them was American-born.

Roque Gonzalez y de Santa-Cruz was the son of noble Spanish parents, and he came into this world at Asunción, the

[2] Quoted by V. F. O'Daniel, O.P., in his *Dominicans in Early Florida* (New York, United States Catholic Historical Society, 1930).

capital of Paraguay, in 1576. He was an unusually good and religious boy, and we are told that some of his companions who did not share his fervor used to throw clods of earth at him when he was saying his prayers in some quiet corner. Later on, when he was about fifteen, he ran away from home with three or four other lads intending to become hermits in the mountains. They had covered thirty miles before they were fetched back. Everybody took it for granted that young Roque would become a priest, and he was in fact ordained when he was twenty-three; but unwillingly, for he felt very strongly that he was unworthy of priesthood.

At once he began to take an interest in the Indians of Paraguay, seeking them out in remote places to preach to and instruct them in Christianity; and aften ten years, to avoid ecclesiastical promotion and to get more opportunity for missionary work, he joined the Society of Jesus.

These were the days of the beginnings of the famous "reductions" of Paraguay, in the formation of which Father Roque Gonzalez played an important part. These remarkable institutions were settlements of Christian Indians run by the Jesuit missionaries, who looked on themselves, not as so many other Spaniards did, as the conquerors and bosses of the Indians, but as the guardians and trustees of their welfare. To the Jesuits, the Indians were not a subservient or "lower" race, but simply untutored children of God; they had no contempt for their civilization and life, in so far as these were not at variance with the gospel of Christ; the missionaries sought to make them Christian Indians and not imitation Spaniards.

The Jesuits' opposition to Spanish imperialism, to slavery

by the colonists, and to the methods of the Inquisition eventually brought about their own downfall in Spanish America and the dissolution of the reductions, more than a century after Father Roque's death. Even the scoffing Voltaire had been impressed, and he wrote that, "When the Paraguayan missions left the hands of the Jesuits in 1678 they had arrived at what is perhaps the highest degree of civilization to which it is possible to lead a young people. . . . In those missions law was respected, morals were pure, a happy brotherliness bound men together, the useful arts and even some of the more graceful sciences flourished, and there was abundance everywhere."

It was to bring about such a happy state of things that Father Roque labored for nearly twenty years, grappling patiently and without discouragement with hardships, dangers, and reverses of all kinds, with intractable and fierce tribes, and with the open opposition of many European colonists. He threw himself heart and soul into the work. For three years he was in charge of the Reduction of St. Ignatius, the first of them, and then spent the rest of his life establishing other reductions, half a dozen in all, east of the Paraná and Uruguay rivers; he was the first European known to have penetrated into some sections of South America. A contemporary Spaniard, the governor of Corrientes, testified from his knowledge of the country that "he was able to appreciate how much the life that Father Roque led must have cost him —hunger, cold, exhaustion from traveling on foot, swimming across rivers, wading through bogs, not to mention plaguing insects and the discomforts which no man but a true apostle, who was holy as this priest was, could have borne with such fortitude."

Father Roque attained an extraordinary influence among the Indians, but his work was hampered in his last years by the attempt of the civil authorities to use this influence for their own ends. They insisted on having their representatives at the new reductions; and the brutality of these aroused in the Indians bitter resentment and suspicion of all Europeans. It is a situation that in one form or another is only too common in missionary history—the work of devoted missionaries being undone by the behavior of less worthy Christians.

In 1628 Father Roque was joined by two young Spanish Jesuits, Alonso (Alphonsus) Rodriguez and Juan (John) de Castillo, and together they founded a new reduction near the Ijuhi River, dedicated in honor of our Lady's Assumption. Father Castillo was left in charge there, while the other two pushed on to Caaró (in the southern tip of what is now Brazil), where they established the All Saints' reduction.

Here they were faced with the hostility of a powerful "medicine man," and at his instigation the mission was soon attacked by a local chief. Father Roque was getting ready to hang a small church bell, when the raiding party arrived. One man stole up from behind and killed him with blows on the head from a tomahawk. Father Rodriguez heard the noise and, coming to the door of his hut to see what it was about, met the blood-stained savages, who knocked him down. "What are you doing, my sons?" he exclaimed. But he was silenced by further blows.

The wooden chapel was set on fire and the two bodies

thrown into the flames. It was November 15, 1628. Two
days later the mission at Ijuhi was attacked. Father Castillo
was seized and bound, barbarously beaten, and stoned to
death.

The first steps toward the beatification of these heroic
missionaries were taken within six months of their martyrdom, by the writing down of evidence about what had happened. But these precious documents were lost, apparently on
their way to Rome, and for two hundred years no progress
could be made; it seemed that their cause must fail. Then, to
the joy of all, copies of the originals were found in Argentina,
and on January 25, 1934, Roque Gonzalez, Alonso Rodriguez, and Juan de Castillo were solemnly declared blessed
by Pope Pius XI.

Among these ancient documents was the evidence of an
Indian chief, Guarecupi, that "all the Christians among my
countrymen loved the Father [Roque] and grieved for his
death, because he was the father of us all, and so he was
called by all the Indians of the Paraná."

3

THE ROSE AND
THE LILY

ℰ◊ℛ

S T. ROSE DE FLORES Y OLIVA, "the Rose of
Lima," and St. Mariana de Paredes y Flores, "the Lily
of Quito," are respectively the first and the latest, until now,
of the canonized saints of the Western Hemisphere. They
were nearly contemporary—Rose died the year before Mariana was born; they both were of Spanish parentage and spent
their lives in Peru; and there are very marked points of
resemblance in those lives.

Rose was born at Lima in 1586 and was christened Isabel.
There is a story that in her babyhood some sort of supernatural appearance, "a mystical rose," was seen on her face;
but it would seem that her pet name of Rose was simply due
to her ruddy complexion and graceful features; in that name
she was confirmed by St. Toribio, Archbishop of Lima. As a
child her patience and goodness were extraordinary; she vol-
untarily ate no fruit, and three days a week fasted on bread
and water. One day her mother having put on her head a
garland of flowers, to show her off before some visitors, Rose
stuck a pin so deeply into it that she could not take off the
garland without some difficulty. When she had heard people

23

comment on her prettiness, she rubbed her face with pepper
to inflame her eyes and make her skin blotchy; and when a
woman had admired the fineness of her hands and her shapely
fingers, she rubbed them with lime, and was unable to dress
herself for a month in consequence. By these and other austerities even more surprising in one so young, the child pre-
pared herself for a life that was to be wholly of that pattern.

Rose appears to have had a better education than most
Peruvian girls at that time, and she learned to play musical
instruments and to write verse. But after her father had lost
money in a mining project she had to work by day in the garden and late at night with her needle to help support the
family. Her parents, of course, wanted her to marry; she had
a long struggle with them over this, and eventually gained
her point. Inspired by the example of St. Catherine of Siena,
she became a Dominican tertiary when she was twenty; and
in a cabin in the garden of her parents' house she lived almost
like a recluse. Here she passed long hours in prayer, the
mosquitoes which buzzed round her head making a sort of
musical accompaniment to her praise; and when she spoke of
God the tone of her voice and her sparkling face showed the
fire that burned within her. Concealed on her head she wore a
thin metal circlet, studded on the inside with little sharp
prickles, like a crown of thorns.

Many extraordinary graces are recorded of St. Rose, but
she had also much to suffer from human unkindness and failure to understand her way of life, as well as the even more
severe trial of interior desolation and anguish in her soul. She
was assaulted with violent temptations, but the only help she
got from those she consulted was the recommendation to eat

and sleep more; at length she was examined by a commission of clergy and physicians, who decided that her experiences, good and bad, were supernatural. But it is permissible to think that some of them, if correctly reported, were due to natural physical and psychological causes. Rose wanted to evangelize the Indians, even though, as she thought, they would eat her; but she was called to work for her neighbor by prayer and whatever she could do around her own home for the poor and the sick. Among her charitable efforts was the help she gave to a religious to overcome his addiction to tobacco.

The last three years of Rose's life were spent under the roof of a government official and his wife, who was very fond of her. In their house she was stricken by her last illness, and under long and painful sickness it was her prayer, "Lord, increase my sufferings, and with them increase your love in my heart." She died on August 24, 1617, at the age of thirty-one, and all the great ones of Lima were among the crowds that flocked to her funeral. St. Rose was canonized in 1671, and declared patroness of South America and the Philippines.

Fourteen months after the death of St. Rose, Mariana de Paredes was born at Quito, then in Peru but now of course the capital of Ecuador. Her parents died when she was very young, and she was brought up in the home of her elder sister. Like Rose, her childhood was marked by a precocious piety, so much so that she was allowed to make her first communion at seven—an unusually early age in those days. It was at just this age that St. Teresa of Avila ran away with her little brother Rodrigo to convert the Moors. So Mariana: at twelve she and some playmates planned to go and preach to the

Japanese; and when this adventure was stopped, they—again like Teresa and Rodrigo—changed their ambition and wanted to be hermits in the wilderness.

Mariana's guardians were rather alarmed at the adventurous turn her piety was taking, and they thought it would be safer for her to try her vocation in a convent. But although the necessary arrangements were twice made, something happened unexpectedly each time to prevent their being carried out: the finger of God was seen in this, and Mariana remained at home. Here—again like St. Rose, and with the approval of her Jesuit confessor—she lived as a recluse, not in a separate cabin but in her own apartment in the house. She never went outdoors except to go to church, and she inflicted on herself austerities which, as Father Herbert Thurston, s.j., says, "can only be regarded as horrifying when practiced by a frail young girl delicately reared"; or, as may well be thought, horrifying in any circumstances.

In addition to the ordinary hair shirt, Mariana wore chains and a spiked girdle wound around her body and limbs; and on Fridays she would suspend herself by hair and wrists to a cross fixed to the wall, and there hang for two hours or more. She reduced her food to almost nothing, and eventually is said to have ceased to drink altogether, the better to realize Christ's thirst on the cross: in very hot weather she would raise a glass of water to her lips and then put it down untasted. Three hours in the twenty-four was her allowance of sleep, the rest of her time being devoted to prayer and other religious exercises, according to a rigidly mapped-out timetable. Every Friday night she slept in a coffin, which at other times she kept in her room with a dummy corpse in it, lest she should ever be unmindful of death.

In 1645 there were earthquakes and a serious epidemic in Quito, and Mariana, moved by a sermon she had heard during Lent, offered herself publicly as a victim for the sins of the people. Shortly after, the epidemic began to lessen in virulence; but Mariana was taken ill, and on May 26 she died, at the age of only twenty-six. There was a great outburst of popular devotion, for the people of Quito looked on her as their deliverer and remembered the many spiritual graces and supernatural gifts that had been attributed to her. Nevertheless, it was not until two centuries later that Mariana was beatified, and nearly another hundred years passed before, in 1950, she was canonized.

It cannot be denied that there are difficult features in the lives of such saints as St. Rose of Lima and St. Mariana of Quito. We must believe that, in spite of certain appearances to the contrary, they did not morbidly seek suffering for its own sake, but sought only more closely to unite themselves with our Saviour in His passion and to expiate the shortcomings of those who do no penance. But we are not bound to believe that their austerities and other religious observances were always prudently chosen: an heroic love of God and holiness of character can express themselves in good ways and in ways that are not so good. There is no disrespect in having misgivings—not to use a stronger word—about some of the things that we are told about St. Rose and St. Mariana and other saints (Blessed Martin de Porres and the dropsical friar, for example).

An Anglo-Colombian writer, Edward Sarmiento, writing

on the life of the mystics, points out that people like St. Rose
of Lima and St. Mariana of Quito seem "to have had a
capacity for living in almost a vacuum." "The admiring but
ordinary Christian," he says, "even supposing he had the
courage to deny self so consistently," as Rose and Mariana
did, would be puzzled how to set about such a program of
self-annihilation. It would seem impossible to do it in the
world we know, short of climbing "to the top of a very tall
column and quietly settling down to starve"—a very different
effect from that produced on the reader by the life of, say, that
queen of mystics, the Spanish St. Teresa. There is a great
diversity of vocations, and some are only for the very few.
And there are things in the lives of many saints which, as
wise old Alban Butler used to say two centuries ago, are matter for wonder rather than for imitation; were the ordinary
Christian to try to copy them, only harm and scandal would
result. It is the spirit of holiness, the pure love of God, that
matters, and for these Rose and Mariana were canonized.

4

A MOHAWK MAIDEN

APART from the martyrs of the seventeenth century the three saints and *beatae* of North America are all women. I don't think there is any special significance in that; there are not lacking male candidates also for the honors of sainthood. But it so happens that among these other candidates the one whose cause is farthest advanced is again a woman. And she is of special importance and interest because she was an Indian, what in England we always distinguish as a Red Indian.

If I were writing about Kateri Tekakwitha for English readers I should have to say something about those Red Indians, because what little we English know about them is mostly faint memories of what we read in the romances of Fenimore Cooper and the like when we were young; and I suspect the generation after mine has hardly even that. In any case, Fenimore Cooper is not much help, for he was concerned with those aspects of the Indians and their life that are of lesser importance where Kateri is concerned. You Americans are in a different position. The Indians were the original inhabitants of your country; the history of the European settlers is all mixed up with them—sometimes frighteningly, sometimes shamefully; you have their descendants living among you to this day. The Indians are part of your American history, and there is no need for me, a foreigner, to say anything more about them.

Except this. That a great deal of the importance and interest of Kateri Tekakwitha comes from her Indian background and the history of her people; and to think of her as a copper-colored child of Indian parents who, upon receiving the universal religion of Jesus Christ, became a sort of "European, or white American, by adoption" would be altogether wrong. This is most clearly brought out in Dr. Daniel Sargent's splendid *Catherine Tekakwitha,* published in 1936. Of the 244 pages of that book, two thirds or more are devoted to the Indians, their history, religion, and social life, and the coming of the first Christian missionaries—mostly French Jesuits—among them.

In October 1646 St. Isaac Jogues and St. John Lalande suffered martyrdom at the Mohawk village of Ossernenon, now Auriesville in Montgomery County, New York State. Ten years later there was born at that same place a girl child who received the name of Tekakwitha. Her father was a Mohawk sachem, her mother an Algonquin, commonly said to have been a war captive. The mother had been baptized, but both parents died of smallpox when Tekakwitha was four; she came under the charge of an uncle, and grew up like any other Mohawk girl. She herself had had smallpox, and was marked by it for life, with also that weakness of sight which the disease so often leaves.

After the epidemic the village was moved up the Mohawk River to Kanawaka, and when a peace was made after French troops had burned Kanawaka in 1666, the Black Robes—Christian priests, Jesuits—appeared in the village. A chapel

was built, some remarkable conversions were made, and in 1675, when she was nearly nineteen, Tekakwitha herself was baptized. She was given the name of Catherine, after the virgin martyr of Alexandria.[1]

Hitherto, it seems, Tekakwitha had taken no part at all in the Christian movement at Kanawaka; what she had done— and we have no information as to how it came about—was to resolve to remain single. After baptism she very soon became The Christian of the village, and those who opposed this new religion made a dead set at her, especially when she refused

[1] I suppose Kateri to be the Indian version of this name, and it is to be hoped Americans will keep to it. In any case Catherine is a French form: Katharine, or Katherine, is the traditional English spelling.

to work in the fields on Sundays and other holy days. Eventually, with the help of a Christian Huron and a Christian Mohawk (called her brother-in-law, since he had married a girl from Tekakwitha's long house), she slipped away and made her way 300 miles to the Christian Indian village which the Jesuits had established at Caughnawaga, around a bend of the Saint Lawrence from Montreal.

Here Kateri found the people divided religiously into three groups: the unbaptized learners, or catechumens; the baptized neophytes, doing as it were a novitiate; and those who were obtaining a higher degree of proficiency in Christian life. She was quickly admitted to the third of these, and at Christmas 1677 Kateri made her first communion—a day of more than usual solemnity and rejoicing, for these Indian converts were not admitted to communion, the Supper, the heart of the Sacrifice, till at least two years after they had undertaken to "put on a new man" at baptism.

One of the reasons for the establishment of the village at Caughnawaga was in order that Indian Christians be able to go on living as Indians, economically, culturally, socially, so far as their former heathen religion was not involved. The civil authorities of New France wanted to turn the Indians into "Christian Frenchmen"; but the Jesuits knew better than that, whether theoretically or practically. Purged of its heathenism, there was nothing wrong with the Indian way of life; and the Jesuits agreed with an Algonquin who said that an Indian couldn't be turned into a Frenchman unless he changed skins with a Frenchman. And so Kateri was able to go on living the life to which she was accustomed. She lodged in a long house in the care of a widow, Anastasia, who had known her parents; she dressed as she had always done, but gave up braiding her hair with wampum ornaments; she worked in the fields and did a lumberjack's job in the forest; she went on hunting trips with the men, praying before two crossed twigs in a glade of the forest at the hour when Mass was being celebrated back home in Caughnawaga. And she made a friend, Mary Tegaiagenta, a widow and a penitent drunkard. (Drunkenness was one of the besetting vices of the Indians, male and female, as Blessed Philippine Duchesne discovered with horror.)

Soon after its foundation by Blessed Margaret Bourgeoys, Kateri visited the convent at Montreal; and it seems to have been due to Tegaiagenta that she conceived the idea of an Indian convent on an island of the Saint Lawrence. Nothing came of it, as nothing could come of it at that stage. But Teka-kwitha and Tegaiagenta, together with a third, the Huron Mary Skarighions, lived as much like nuns as they could, praying together and practicing austerities in a way that came naturally to Indians, with their "stoic" traditions. Neverthe-less, circumstances—and not least the Indian social setup— pointed to marriage for Kateri; and her "aunt," Anastasia, tried to persuade her to it. But Kateri refused with firmness, even obstinacy. Father Cholenc supported her, and on the feast of the Annunciation in 1677 Kateri made a vow of per-petual virginity. (What a pity we have forgotten the lovely English word "maidenhood.") It was no doubt the first time a North American Indian girl had done such a thing in the history of the world.

On April 17, 1680, Kateri died, after ailing and suffering for several months. She was twenty-three years old. Kateri

Tekakwitha was, Father Cholenc tells us, always gay, always content. As he says, that was surprising, for gaiety is not a characteristic we look for in a Mohawk. And he adds that the other Indians liked to be near her in the chapel "so that they could pray better."

A certain friend of Kateri, Father Chauchtière, had several visions of her after her death. He believed she told him to make her picture, and he did his best to draw it from memory. The picture was engraved in 1742, and so we can see it today reproduced in Dr. Sargent's book. It does not make Kateri look particularly like an Indian, and the attitude is stilted and artificial—redolent of seventeenth-century France. But it is nice to have it. It is difficult to "think ourselves back" into so unfamiliar a life as hers.We know more about it than might be expected and much less than we should like. But it seems clear that, with more than 3,000 miles and 200 years and an infinity of external difference separating them, Kateri Teka-kwitha belonged to the company of St. Thérèse of Lisieux, followers of "the little way."

5

ST. TORIBIO

I WONDER how many people outside of South America have ever heard of St. Toribio.[1] And yet he is, equally with St. Rose of Lima, the first known saint of the New World. It is true that he was not born on the American continent, and not canonized by the Church until fifty-five years after her, but they lived in the same place at the same time. Toribio died first, and it was he who conferred the sacrament of confirmation on Rose.

Toribio Alfonso Mogrobejo was born in Spain in 1538. His childhood and youth were notably religious, but he had no intention of becoming a priest and was, in fact, educated for the law. He was so brilliant a scholar that he became professor of law in the famous university of Salamanca. While there he attracted the notice of King Philip II of Spain (widower of Queen Mary I of England), and eventually the king made him chief judge of the ecclesiastical court of the Inquisition at Granada. This was a surprising position for a layman to hold, and it was not a pleasant or easy post for anyone, layman or cleric. But it led to something even more surprising. After some years the archbishopric of Lima, in the Spanish colony of Peru, became vacant. Toribio had carried out his

1 The Latin form, St. Turibius, is also used.

judge's duties so well, and displayed such a fine missionary spirit, that it was decided to send him to Peru as archbishop.

Toribio was shocked at this decision, and wrote to the royal council pointing out that he was entirely unfitted for the office, and that anyway it was against canon law to appoint a layman to ecclesiastical dignities. The council replied that they were better judges of his fitness than he was, and as for his second objection, that would easily be gotten over: he would have to be ordained priest and bishop. So Toribio submitted. He was consecrated bishop, and in 1581 landed in Peru. He was then forty-three years old.

Like similar enterprises by other nations elsewhere, the immediate effects of Spanish conquest and colonization in South America were not all evil, and were very far from being all good. With the Europeans came Christianity, and the Church's missionaries achieved much—in some places more than in others—for the spiritual and temporal welfare of the native Indians; they would have done even more but for the tight control of the Spanish civil authorities. But a worse handicap was the behavior of so many of the conquerors. With whatever individual exceptions, they were filled with a lust for wealth, exploiting and pillaging the country, enslaving the people and making them work in the mines for the benefit of their oppressors.

St. Toribio arrived in Peru not quite fifty years after Pizarro's conquest, and he was indeed faced with a tough proposition. Not only was religion in decay among the officials, the military and the colonists; but also, it must be sadly admitted, some of the clergy who had come out from Spain to spread the good news of Christ had failed to withstand the

dangers and temptations of their new surroundings. The archbishop decided at once to make a visitation of his whole territory, which was huge. It stretched 400 miles or more along
the Pacific Coast and many miles inland among the spurs of
the Andes, some 18,000 square miles in all; with no means
of transportation except horses and mules, and often not even
these. That first visitation, which he was to repeat twice more,
took him seven years to complete.

It was not only the wildness and roughness of the country,
and the rigors of the climate bringing on sickness, that made
progress slow. "Time is not our own: we shall have to give a
strict account of it," was a favorite saying of St. Toribio. This
meant that he must not hurry unduly, for the work that he
had to do needed care and patience; were he to hurry through
it, and then rush off to somewhere else, he would be wasting
his time.

Among the things that took time was the study of the
Indian languages and dialects. It was one of the troubles in
Peru (and elsewhere) that Indians were often baptized who
had hardly any knowledge of the Christian faith and its obli-
gations. One reason for this was that many missionaries had
very little knowledge of the Indian languages. St. Toribio at
once saw the difficulty and tried to remedy it, beginning with
himself.

Naturally enough their new archbishop was not popular
among many of the Spaniards, the wickedness of whose lives
he reproved and whose oppression of the Indians he opposed;
they did all they could to hamper him. And they could do a
lot, for St. Toribio was no respecter of persons and was as
quick to condemn an influential citizen as an unimportant one;

so he had opponents in high places. When he wanted to stop a public abuse he did not simply say from the pulpit, "It is wrong to do so-and-so." He would say, "Don X. Y. Z. persists in doing so-and-so. This is wicked; and if he does not know why, I will tell him." Then as now, offenders tried to wriggle out of it. "What's the harm?" they would say. "Everybody does it." And Toribio would reply with a quotation from one of the early defenders of the Church, Tertullian: "Our Lord said, 'I am the truth.' He did not say, 'I am the custom.'"

In spite of opposition, St. Toribio's twenty-five years as archbishop of Lima were full of achievements. In 1591 he founded the first seminary in the New World, at Lima. He established churches, religious houses, hospitals, and schools, and in civil affairs he gave special encouragement to the making of roads—he, more than anybody, knew how much they were needed. Every two years he assembled his clergy round him in council, and the difficulties of travel were sometimes made an excuse for not attending.

As a missionary he was no less successful, and he is said to have baptized and confirmed half a million souls. Figures like that are completely unreliable and almost certainly exaggerated, but we may be sure it was a large number. Among those he confirmed, as well as St. Rose, are said to have been Blessed Martin de Porres and Blessed John Massias. From 1590 he had the help of another great missionary, the Franciscan St. Francis Solano, whose denunciations of the wickedness of Lima so alarmed the people that the viceroy had to call on St. Toribio to calm them.

Toribio made so strong an appeal to the Indians partly

because of his knowledge of their languages, which he kept on studying almost up to his death. But even more it was because of his shining goodness and his obvious concern for their welfare. In order to have time to instruct them properly he would stay for days in villages where he could hardly get food, much less a bed. When he heard of Indians lost in the mountains he would himself brave the hardships and dangers of the rescue parties searching for them; and always he did all he could to lighten their burden of poverty and oppression. On his most arduous journeys he would celebrate Mass every day, and daily confess to his chaplain. For St. Toribio love of God and love of his spiritual children always went hand in hand, and he did not forget that their bodies were the dwelling place of their souls.

He was no less selfless in caring for his Spanish flock. In Lima he was a frequent visitor to the hospitals, taking comfort and the sacraments to the patients; he helped the victims of epidemics at great cost to himself; and he encouraged public processions of penitence—a common feature of Spanish religious life—walking in them himself. He had feeling for the sensitive pride of his people. He knew that many are shy about making their poverty or their other needs known; they do not like to accept public charity or help from their acquaintances. So he did all he could to assist them privately, without their knowing from whom their benefactions came.

St. Toribio's last sickness attacked him when he was away from Lima, at Pacasmayo, far to the north. Working to the last, he struggled as far as Santa, where he knew the end was at hand. He made his will, giving his personal belongings to his servants and all the rest of his property for the benefit of the poor. He asked to be carried to the church to receive viaticum there, and was then brought back to bed and anointed. While those about him sang the psalm, "I was glad when they said unto me, We will go into the house of the Lord," St. Toribio died, on March 23, 1606. He was sixty-eight years old.

It has been said of him that he renewed the face of the Church in Peru. His influence was felt beyond those borders, so that his feast is now kept all over South America. St. Rose of Lima, on the other hand, is the patron saint of the continent, and her feast is kept in all parts of the world. Perhaps that is why she is so much better known than St. Toribio. But in remembering the one, we ought not to forget the other.

6

THE TERESA OF CANADA

❧

AMONG those the cause of whose beatification has been
begun is a woman who, though she was French "to the
tips of her fingers," spent the last thirty years of her life in
Canada; and of whom the chiefs and braves of the Huron
nation wrote to Pope Pius IX two centuries after her death:

> She it was who called us from the depths of our forests to
> teach us to know and worship the true Lord of life. . . . Many
> moons have gone by since that first dawning of the true light
> upon us. Our nation was great then; it is now threatened with
> complete extinction. And we beg you, Holy Father, to receive
> with the last greeting and the last breath of the Huron tribe the
> testimony of its deep gratitude to the reverend Mother Mary of
> the Incarnation.

Mary Guyard was born in 1599 at Tours in France, where
her father was a baker. When she was fourteen she declared
her wish to be a nun. But her parents did not agree: they
thought her too merry and attractive for the religious life,
and so arranged a marriage for her with a young man named
Claude Martin. She accepted it obediently and cheerfully (she
was then eighteen), and lived very happily with her husband,
although she had a dragon of a mother-in-law. A boy was
born, and then, after two years, Claude Martin suddenly died.

He left his business thoroughly "in the red." Mary, who testified herself that she had "a talent for trade," as she certainly had, set herself to get it out. And at this very moment God chose to speak to her in a special way. One day she was going down the street about her affairs, murmuring to herself, "Lord, I have trusted in thee: do not let me be finally overcome," when she suddenly had a most vivid sense of the horror of sin and of what the Son of God had done for mankind. Mary had always been a sincerely religious girl, but from this moment, she says, "I was so mightily changed that I no longer knew myself."

But there was no outward change in her manner of life. She paid off her husband's debts, and then went with her little boy to housekeep for her sister and her husband, who had a big carrier's business. And so well did she manage this large and unruly household that after a few years her brother-in-law made her in effect general manager and factotum of his business. In these surroundings, in the company of tough porters and drivers, with fifty or sixty horses in her care, Mary developed a deep and remarkable spiritual life. As Father James Brodrick says, "One likes to think of those great, patient, shaggy-footed beasts being rubbed down and given their oats by one of the grandest mystics in history."

An outstanding quality of Mary Martin at this time was her motherliness in relation to the score of rough workmen into whose company she was thrown: "They flew to her in all their troubles, and she flew to them when they fell ill." This adds significance to the great crisis that came to her when she had been ten years a widow. The call to the religious life was so loud in her ears that she determined to answer it, though it

meant parting from her adored and adoring eleven-year-old son, Claude. The break and its circumstances are harrowing even to read about. Forty years later Mary wrote to him from Canada (Claude was then one of the best-known Benedictine monks in France): "I tell you again that in separating from you I subjected myself to a living death. . . . At parting from you it seemed as if my soul was being wrenched from my body."

The Abbé Bremond, who writes so brilliantly and enthusiastically about Mary, is indeed a little troubled as to whether she ought to have left her son so young. "I prefer a clear duty to an uncertain one, and I think I should have forbidden her to leave the boy." But, he adds, "I also think that I should have been disturbed by the old warning, 'Cursed is he who measures the things of God by the standards of man: cursed is he who sets aside the inspirations of Heaven for the uncertain voice of the flesh.' "

Mary Guyard, *veuve* Martin, entered the Ursuline convent of Tours on the feast of the Annunciation, 1631; henceforward she was Sister Mary of the Incarnation. (She must not be confused with that other French Mary of the Incarnation, "the beautiful Mrs. Acarie," who, after attaining holiness in the married state, passed her last three years as a Carmelite, died in 1618, and was beatified in 1791). At this time Sister Mary had never heard of a country called Canada; but at Christmas, 1634, she had a curious dream, which the Jesuit Father Dinet interpreted as a call to work there. At the same time she read a report from the superior of the Jesuits in North America, Father Paul le Jeune, in which he hoped for the establishment in Quebec of a school for Indian girls, "under the direction of some brave mistress, some Amazon," whom Almighty God might call from Europe for the work. This settled Sister Mary. But there ensued a long and mighty tussle between her and her former director, Father Raymund de Saint-Bernard, a Cistercian monk. For he, good man, wanted to go to Canada himself, but firmly and fiercely averred that it was no place for women—converting Red Indians was a job for men only. This episode, of which considerable records survive, shows the spirit and good humor, the single-mindedness and holy determination of Sister Mary at their best. Of course she won, and Father Raymund himself never got to Canada. But it was not till five years after her dream that Sister Mary set out on her three months' voyage, together with two other Ursulines.

Their first home in Quebec was two rickety birchbark cabins in the Lower Town, near Champlain's *Habitation*. These had to shelter eighteen people—three nuns, several French girls, and the rest Indian children. The habits of the last were stupefying by good French *bourgeois* standards; they would put their filthy moccasins in the cooking pot, their heads were alive with vermin, and they stank abominably. But Sister Mary's motherliness came into play again, and she delighted in the little ragamuffins: they reminded her, somewhat obscurely, of "early Christians." The nuns had to live thus for three years, until their convent, paid for by a wealthy Norman widow, Madeleine de la Peltrie, was built. Smallpox ravaged their pupils; supplies of food and clothing from France often failed to arrive; Iroquois raided the missions, and then Mary Martin of the Tours transport days came into her own, and she humped muskets and ammunition for the garrison with the best. In 1650 the new convent—on the same site that the Ursuline convent is today—was burned down. But whatever or whoever was "down" it was never Mother Mary.

Indian languages are very difficult for Europeans. St. Noel Chabanel, the martyr, was one who could never learn them, however hard he tried. In twenty years Mother Mary mastered Huron, Algonquian, and Iroquois so thoroughly as to be able to write catechisms, prayer books, and Bible histories in them, as well as a dictionary. Everybody came to her for advice and help, and she knew personally all the North American martyrs; she said of St. Gabriel Lalemant that he was the most holy man she had ever known. And amid all her work and worries to write to her son Claude was always a first charge (she was as wonderful a letter writer as Claude was a tedious one). In one letter to him, carried by a friend who was returning to France, she says, "I lifted my veil for him, so that he could tell you he has seen me as well as talked to me."

Father Brodrick's words that Mother Mary was "one of the grandest mystics in history" have been quoted. Her printed spiritual and other writings already fill four volumes, and half of the sixth volume of Abbé Bremond's history of French spirituality is devoted to her. She spoke in the most persuasive way of the truths of Christianity and had a genius for religious teaching; and her wisdom and eloquence were the fruit of the Holy Spirit in her devoted life. The Bible was almost her only book, and she had very little time for study. Nevertheless, she wrote,

Abundant light was granted me, and my mind received a gift of wisdom which sometimes prompted me to say things that otherwise I should not have wanted or dared to say. . . . I was astonished at the number of relevant passages from the Bible that came to me. I could not but speak. I had to obey the spirit that dwelt in me. . . .

In her convent at Quebec, Mother Mary encouraged devotion to the Sacred Heart of Jesus some time before the revelations of St. Margaret Mary; and the first celebration of the feast of the Sacred Heart in the New World took place in that convent on June 18, 1700, twenty-eight years after her death, which happened on April 30, 1672. She was seventy-three.

The famous French preacher Bossuet called Mary of the Incarnation "the Teresa of her time and of the New World," referring to the great Spanish mystic and Carmelite foundress. The Church calls her a Venerable Servant of God. Doubtless the time will come when we shall all call her Blessed Mary of Quebec, the merry nun from Touraine.

7

FOUR FRIARS

❦

LET me recall to memory four holy men who had a good deal in common. They were all born in Spain; they were all friars of St. Francis or St. Dominic, two of them after living for a time "in the world"; they all worked in South America; and they died within sixty-five years of one another, three of them in the land of their adoption.

Writing above about St. Toribio, I mentioned his fellow missionary in Peru, St. Francis Solano; and it is this Francis who is the first on my list now. He was born in the middle of the sixteenth century in Andalusia, a part of Spain whose climate and surroundings were in some respects not unlike the distant land where nearly half his life was to be spent. He became a Franciscan when he was twenty, and after his ordination he soon made his mark as a preacher. Two things are especially remembered about Francis in those early years. One was that, when he was master of novices and found his charges in some fault or irregularity, instead of giving them a penance, he gave it to himself. "For," he said, "if they stand in need of correction it must be my fault for not teaching them better." The other was when the city of Granada was stricken by an epidemic of plague in 1583. Father Francis was selfless and fearless in looking after the bodies and souls of the sick, so that he caught the disease himself. But instead of dying, as everybody expected, he made a quick recovery, and directly the epidemic was over he volunteered to go as a missionary among the Moors in Africa. But permission was withheld, and it was not till six years later that he was chosen with others to reinforce the Franciscans not in Africa but in Peru.

The missionaries sailed to Panama, crossed the isthmus where ships now steam through the canal, and again took ship on the other side. But as they drew near to Peru a bad storm sprang up and the vessel was driven aground on a sandbank. She looked as if she would go to pieces, and the master ordered that she be abandoned, leaving aboard a number of Negro slaves for whom there was no room in the only lifeboat. Francis Solano refused to leave them, so he was left behind on the ship. He gathered the Negroes around him (some of them he already had under instruction), encouraged them to trust in God and His divine Son who had died for them, and then baptized them. He had scarcely done this when the ship broke up and some of the Negroes were drowned. The remainder were marooned for three days on the part of the hull that was firmly aground, but Father Francis kept up their courage, and when the weather mended they were taken off and brought safely to Lima.

That was a fitting beginning to the twenty years that St. Francis labored among the Indians and Spanish colonists in South America. The Jesuit who preached his funeral sermon said that God had singled him out to be "the hope and example of all Peru, the model and glory of Lima, the splendor of the Franciscan order." Many miracles were attributed to him, not the least that he had the gift of tongues in the sense of a supernatural ability to make himself understood when preaching to the Indians. This may or may not have been so. What is certain is that it was at this very time that the Archbishop of Lima, St. Toribio Mogrobejo, was insisting that his clergy not try to make Christians of the Indians without knowing their languages; and when Francis Solano was sent across the Andes to Tucuman (now in the Argentine) we are told the first thing he did was to set about learning Indian tongues. Not till then did he set out on a missionary journey through the Chaco to Paraguay, afterward the scene of the famous "reductions" of the Society of Jesus.

But the life of St. Francis was not made up solely of journeys of bewildering difficulty and danger, preaching the gospel to the heathen with sensational results. There was plenty for him to do of another kind among the Peruvian Spaniards in the coastal towns and elsewhere. In 1604 his preaching in the city square against the corruptions of Lima and his comparison of the fate of a sinful soul to that of a doomed city—in the manner of a Hebrew prophet of old—had so powerful an effect that the people panicked. Many, no doubt, were conscience-stricken, but many more were simply frightened out of their wits. They remembered that Father Francis had foretold things before, and they had come true; they expected a calamity was about to come upon them, like Ninive, we should say, but probably few of them had ever heard of Ninive.

Even the viceroy was alarmed, but he was alarmed for public order. He went to the archbishop, St. Toribio, and together they conferred with the superior of the Franciscans. Then St. Francis was sent for and given his instructions. He must go out to the people and calm them by making clear the

meaning of what he had said: he had not prophesied earthquakes and material flames and the destruction of buildings;
he had been telling them what would happen to their souls if
they did not repent and mend their ways. No doubt the people of Lima were very simple folk 350 years ago: but perhaps
it is not unknown for better-educated Christians today sometimes to miss the "spiritual point" and to see only the material
symbols. But we must not, because of this incident, picture St.
Francis as hard and fanatical. He was very fond of music,
and a habit of his was to take his lute and play and sing before
our Lady's statue, which may well remind us of his religious
father and namesake, St. Francis of Assisi.

Ten years before St. Francis Solano died at Lima in 1610
there died in Mexico at a great age—ninety-eight—a Franciscan lay brother named Sebastian Aparicio. He could look
back on a very varied and unusual life. He had been born not
far from Salamanca in Spain, the child of very poor peasants,
and for ten years he earned his living first as a shepherd's boy,
then as a manservant, then as a farm laborer. Twice he left
jobs to avoid occasions of temptation, and finally, when he
was about twenty, he emigrated to America and settled in
Mexico.

From then on it was a case of "poor boy makes good."
Sebastian started a carrying business between Mexico City and
Zacatecas, and it prospered; he enlarged his scope and became
a contractor, especially for the making of roads. By the exercise of the virtues of the frontier he became a wealthy man.
By the exercise of the virtues of the spirit he became a good
man. He gave away much in charity, provided dowries for

girls, bought out debtors, lent money without asking for repayment—no wonder Sebastian was popular. But respected, too: Spaniards and Indians alike brought their disputes to him to be settled. So simply, not to say austerely, did he live that, in spite of his great benefactions, he was able to retire from business when he was fifty. He bought a large ranch and settled down to breed cattle. Then, when he was sixty, he married, apparently to please the relatives of a penniless girl. His wife soon died, and he married again. The second wife also died. Sebastian Aparicio was now seventy.

Then he was taken seriously ill. Hitherto his life had been exemplary, but he took his sickness as a warning that he had not done enough. When he recovered, he made over his property to the Poor Clare nuns and gave his services as well to one of their convents. But even this was not enough. Sebastian offered himself as a lay brother to the Franciscans and was accepted. Eventually he was sent to the big friary at Puebla de los Angeles, where he lived for another quarter of a century, working as if he were still a young man. Much of the work was to do with animals, especially draught animals, mules and oxen mostly; and like many another saint Brother Sebastian showed a remarkable understanding of and influence over dumb beasts. Mules are notoriously intractable creatures, but he could manage them almost without moving his lips or raising a finger. And his power extended to wild animals too.

When he was dying, Blessed Sebastian was unable to swallow, and so could not receive viaticum. But the Body of the Lord was brought to his cell that he might worship it, and in so doing his long life came to its peaceful end on February 25, 1600.

In some respects the life of Blessed John Massias resembles that of Sebastian Aparicio. He, too, was once a shepherd lad in Spain, born in 1585, when Sebastian still had fifteen years to live. But John was not enterprising like the other; he kept on as a shepherd, and during the long hours when there was nothing particular to do except keep his eyes and ears open he would say his rosary over and over again. Sometimes, as he meditated on the mysteries, it seemed to him that the holy ones were there, visible and talking with him; and he said it was because St. John the Evangelist told him to do so that he decided to follow so many of his countrymen to America. Anyway, go to America he did and, after working a couple of years on a farm in Peru, he went to Lima and joined the Dominicans as a lay brother at their priory of St. Mary Magdalen.

A lay brother's life is rarely outwardly eventful, and there is not much known about John's. But all Lima knew him. He was given charge of the door, and his lodge there, like that of his friend Martin de Porres at the other friary in the town, soon became the meeting place for the poor, the sick, and the wretched. He begged alms with which to feed and physic them, and accompanied his relief with advice and encouragement to good living and the love of God. Like St. Toribio before him, John had a sensitive feeling for those who were too shy to beg in person: these he sought out himself in their homes. And to save time in begging from door to door he trained his donkey to go round by itself and receive in its panniers gifts for the poor. St. Mary Magdalen's was a very strict house, but Brother John's voluntary mortifications and penances were such that his superiors had to interfere and restrain his imprudent excesses. He lived to a good age, and when he died in 1645, all Lima, led by the viceroy and the archbishop, followed his body to its grave.

Our fourth friar is the first in order of time, but I have left him till last because only half-a-dozen years of his life were spent in America. This was St. Louis Bertrand, who was ordained priest as a Dominican in 1547 at Valencia in Spain. (He was ordained by another canonized saint, Thomas of Villanova.)

Father Louis was in Colombia and Panama (New Granada it was called then) between 1562 and 1569, and those few years were marked by intense missionary activity among the Indians. The numbers said to have been baptized by Louis Bertrand were very large indeed, and it must be admitted either that the numbers have been exaggerated, or else that many of these conversions were superficial, for we know that St. Louis spoke only Spanish and had to rely on interpreters. But what is certain is that this holy man spent some years of most heroic effort on the American continent, "in journeying often, in perils of waters, in perils of robbers . . . in labor and painfulness"; and even found time to visit some of the Lesser Antilles, where the Caribs tried to poison him. St. Louis was also one of the earlier of those who raised their voice against the avarice, cruelty, and bad example of so many of the Spanish adventurers in America.

Of these four men who contributed in their several ways

to the evangelization of the New World, St. Louis Bertrand was canonized in 1671 and Francis Solano in 1726, Sebastian Aparicio was beatified in 1787 and John Massias in 1837.

8

THE FIRST SCHOOLMISTRESS
OF MONTREAL

⚜

I N THE YEAR 1620, four months before the Pilgrim
Fathers sailed from England, there was born at Troyes
in France a girl child called Margaret Bourgeoys. Her father
was a candle manufacturer in a good way of business, and she
was the sixth in a family of twelve children.

There was nothing very remarkable about Margaret's early
life—her six younger brothers and sisters seem to have kept
her pretty busy. But when she was twenty she offered herself
as a postulant to the Carmelite nuns—and was refused. Then
she tried the Poor Clares—and was again refused. The
superiors' reasons for these refusals are not known. But Margaret's spiritual director, Father Gendret, thought he knew
God's reasons. This good priest had long wanted to organize
an uncloistered community to look after the welfare of young
girls, and surely it was clearly God's will that Margaret
Bourgeoys should be a leader in this work.

But Father Gendret was mistaken. He made a beginning
with Margaret and two others; but very soon the experiment
failed: Margaret went back home, and again took up her work
as president of the local sodality of our Lady. All these

rebuffs must have been very discouraging; but God did not allow Margaret to be discouraged, for one day when she was at prayer He sent her a vision of the Child Jesus. From that moment, she declared, the beauty of the divine Child "turned my eyes forever from all the beauty of this world."

In 1652, when she was thirty-two, Margaret was deeply impressed by a vivid dream in which she saw a man dressed like a country priest. A few days later she was called to the parlor of a local convent, and there she was introduced to a man exactly like the one in her dream. But he was not a priest: he was Paul de Maisonneuve, governor of the little French settlement of Ville Marie where today stands the great city of Montreal. Maisonneuve had a sister in the Troyes convent, and he had asked her to find a schoolmistress for his little colony. Margaret Bourgeoys was suggested. She at once recognized the call of God, and volunteered for the job.

She landed at Quebec on September 22 in the following year. She found it no more than a "fortified township pompously decked out with the name of 'city,'" its struggling inhabitants living in poverty and terrified by the Iroquois Indians (The Venerable Mary of the Incarnation had arrived there a dozen years before). But a month later she found Ville Marie much worse. It was simply a fort on the bank of the Saint Lawrence with a couple of hundred souls all living within its walls; there was a small chapel but no resident priest—a Jesuit missionary was there sometimes. On the one side was the river, on the other the height of Mount Royal, and beyond, the wilderness and the forests—and the Indians.

Margaret Bourgeoys had made that terrible voyage and

come to that desolate, fear-ridden spot to teach the children. But there were at that moment no children of teachable age. So for more than four years Margaret was at everybody's beck and call. She kept house for the governor; she looked after two little girls; she did all she could for the wives of the soldiers of the garrison; she helped Jeanne Mance in her tiny hospital; she brought about the restoration of the great cross on Mount Royal—its predecessor had been destroyed by the Iroquois; she had a new chapel of our Lady of Help almost ready for the arrival of some priests from Saint-Sulpice in Paris in 1657. She was already showing she could get things done.

It was during the next year that her school was at last opened. It was housed in a building that had, appropriately enough, been a stable. There were less than a dozen pupils, girls and boys, and one assistant. But Margaret Bourgeoys was looking ahead. She saw that Ville Marie would grow, and with it her work—and there were the children of the Indians to be kept in mind. Where would she get helpers? There was only one answer to that question; and in the same year she sailed with Jeanne Mance back to France. That was the first of three voyages she made home in the interests of her work: and remember it was a matter of great hardships and many months each time—there were no ocean liners, luxury or not, in those days.

Margaret was away twelve months, and when she got back it was with an old friend from Troyes, Catherine Crolo, and three other volunteers. The years that followed were full of disturbances and alarms because of the Iroquois war; but Margaret and her helpers went on steadily with their work, and added to it: a kindergarten for a few adopted Indian children, household instruction for older girls, and the organization of a sodality of our Lady. There was one period of especially grinding poverty, but Margaret had an immovable trust in the providence of God; and though it sometimes did not seem like it at the time, that trust was amply rewarded. There was a very obvious manifestation of divine power and help one especially cold winter, when ships with supplies from France were long overdue. Daily Margaret prayed as she doled out the small ration of flour from the household's insufficient stock. And as the days went by, that stock appeared never to grow less, until the long-expected ships arrived.

Eventually Margaret was given permission to organize her little community into a religious congregation, and it was recognized by the famous first bishop of Quebec, Msgr. de Laval, in 1676. But this led to new and serious worries. Communities of uncloistered nuns were practically unknown in the Church at that time, and Bishop Laval could not understand why Mother Bourgeoys was not willing to carry on her teaching inside a convent enclosure. She answered all his questions and objections, and humbly but very firmly pointed out that the vocation of herself and her sisters was a *missionary* vocation, and that monastic enclosure would make it impossible for their work to be carried on. The bishop did not insist. But when he died, his successor, Bishop de Saint-Vallier, who was a very "difficult" character, brought up all the same objections again. It was not until two years before her death that Margaret Bourgeoys and twenty-three Sisters of Notre Dame were allowed to make their vows (Margaret had taken private vows of virginity and poverty when she was twenty-three).

When we think of trials and difficulties with the ecclesiastical authorities such as this, added to the hardships and dangers of pioneering life in Canada, the achievements of Margaret Bourgeoys are all the more remarkable. Not even the destruction of their convent by fire, when two nuns (one of them her own niece) lost their lives, could discourage her —or, rather, weaken her trust in God. Mother Bourgeoys was the First Schoolmistress of Montreal, and she started the first boarding school as well as the first day schools at Ville Marie itself and at several outlying places on the island of Montreal. These last were temporarily destroyed in 1689, when the Iroquois massacred every man, woman, and child not protected by the walls of the fort.

Mother Bourgeoys' work for the Indians was always close to her heart. In 1676 she sent two sisters to open school in a neighboring Indian village called The Mountain. They had only a wigwam of bark to live in and their pupils were literally "little savages," whose clothes, according to a French visitor, "were the most disgusting I've ever seen." Yet within three years two Indian girls had joined Mother Bourgeoys' community. The year the Indian school was begun was the very year that saw the baptism of the Mohawk girl, Kateri Tekakwitha. And not long after she, with her friend Mary Tegaiagenta, visited the convent. No doubt this visit had a lot to do with Kateri's desire—never fulfilled—to establish a religious community of Indian women on Heron island, opposite Montreal.

But Mother Bourgeoys not only had Indians in her French

community, she had two Americans—and from Puritan New England at that. They were among some colonists who had at different times been carried off in raids by the Abenaki Indians. Brought by their captors to Montreal, they were there ransomed by the French, and several of them, inspired by the devotion and lovingness of Margaret Bourgeoys, became Catholics. Two joined the sisters of Notre Dame, and were the first New England ever to become nuns. Their names are worth remembering: Lydia Longley, of Groton, Massachusetts, and Mary G. Sayward, of York, Maine.

For nearly fifty years Margaret Bourgeoys was the most influential, we may say the most important, woman in Montreal. And she "being dead, yet speaketh"; for the community of five souls that began teaching in a disused stable, with a handful of children, has grown into a great congregation, with more than 3,000 sisters and 60,000 pupils in 200 educational establishments of all kinds in North America.

It has been said that women like Margaret Bourgeoys need no fine words: "Their best praise is the record of their deeds, written without comment." I have said a little about some of her deeds, and a little about her troubles and trials. Perhaps the greatest of them was not from outside, but something within herself. She had to struggle against two paralyzing doubts: doubt of her own ability to do what she was called on to do, and a gnawing sense of her unworthiness before God. Her answer was courage and confidence, confidence that God who called her would sustain her. And all the time she was urged on by devotion to the good of the children—and the good of all her neighbors. "I want at all costs," she said, "not only to love my neighbor, but to keep him in love for me."

Her death was as selfless as her life. In December, 1699, the novice mistress of the convent was very ill; and on the last day of the year the aged foundress offered her own life for hers. The young nun got better. But on January 12, 1700, Mother Bourgeoys died. She was eighty years old. One hundred and fifty years later, when Montreal had become a great port with a million inhabitants, Pope Pius XII solemnly declared Margaret to be Blessed. It was the third beatification of a woman who had come from Europe to give her life to North America.

9

AN AMERICAN HERMIT

❧

THE MAN called Gregory Lopez has never been beatified, but at one time—and still, for all I know—he was venerated all over Mexico, and he is always called Blessed Gregory Lopez. Lopez apparently was not his proper name; he seems to have taken it as a disguise. What his real name was we don't know, neither do we know anything about his family or background, except that they must have been people of good position in Spain, for Gregory was well educated, and in his youth he was a page at the court of King Philip II. Later on, when questioned about this, he said, "God only is my father since I took up a new way of life. My brothers must all be dead by this time."

In the year 1562, when he was twenty, Gregory went on a pilgrimage to the Spanish shrine of Our Lady of Guadalupe; and it is supposed that when he was there he was told about that other shrine of Our Lady of Guadaloupe, far away in Mexico, where thirty years before the Mother of God was said to have appeared to the Indian boy, Juan Diego. For Gregory suddenly made up his mind to cross the Atlantic, because he was convinced that that was what God wanted him to do, though why he did not know.

He landed at Vera Cruz and made his way first to Mexico

City and then to Zacatecas; but he did not like either of those places, where the lives of so many people were entirely given up to trying to make themselves rich out of the silver mines. He was seeking the riches of God, not worldly wealth. And when he had seen two men kill each other in a quarrel about money he moved on until he came to a lonely valley, where he settled down as a hermit. The local Indians were at bitter enmity with the Spaniards, but they did no harm to Gregory; on the contrary, they helped him build his hut and brought him food, for he was so quiet and inoffensive and friendly, passing his time in prayer and tilling the soil.

The nearest church was twenty-five miles away, and to it Gregory used to walk on great feasts to assist at Mass and receive the sacraments. But soon he learned that some of the Spaniards were gossiping about him, because they were shocked that he chose to live so far from men that he could go to Mass only at irregular intervals. They forgot how many holy hermits in the history of the Church had lived in just that way. But Gregory did not want to shock anybody or appear to set a bad example; so he left his hermitage and went to work on a plantation nearer a church.

After an earthquake in 1566 Gregory went back to his hermit's life, till at the end of five years he was persuaded by a famous missionary, Father Dominic de Salazar, to "try his vocation" with the Dominicans in Mexico City. Of course community life was the last thing to suit a man like Gregory Lopez; after only a few days of it he left the friars and returned to solitude. But people were beginning to talk again, saying all sorts of things about the simple Gregory, making a "mystery man" of him. The archbishop of Mexico felt bound to take notice, and he appointed some clergy to look into it all. When he had heard their report, the archbishop stated in public that Gregory Lopez was a man of remarkable piety and goodness. Thereupon many of those who had criticized him before turned right around and could not say enough in Gregory's praise: he became so popular that he got no peace, and being a humble man it all made him very unhappy.

There were, however, still people who looked on Gregory as a hypocrite and an idler, as a rather dangerous vagabond, who, simply because he was different from other people, must be subversive of good order and religion. So the archbishop had to interfere again. This time he appointed a learned Jesuit, Father Alonzo Sanchez, to examine Gregory. And Father Sanchez summed up his opinion in one sentence: "Your Excellency, compared with this man Lopez I have not yet learned my spiritual A B C."

Then Gregory was taken ill and had to go into the hospital. While he was there he helped the nursing brothers by writing for them a book on pharmacy, for he had learned a great deal from the Indians about herbal remedies and the virtues of plants. When he came out he found a new place of retirement, not far from Michoacan, where he was joined by his friend Don Losa. This priest had given up his position on the staff of the cathedral of Mexico City to be with Gregory Lopez, and the two lived together till Gregory died seven years later.

There was nothing startling about their way of life: it was simple and well ordered, with apparently no exaggerated austerities and observances such as are so often

found in Spanish (and other) records. Their practice of poverty was marked more by a careful use of what was available than by any spectacular "going without"; and Gregory was scrupulously clean in his body and tidy in his clothing, which is more than can be said for some solitaries. "We poor must look after ourselves, so as not to be a nuisance to our neighbors," he would say.

Much of their time was spent in study of the Bible, of which Gregory had an unusual knowledge, both of its text and its meaning. When it was misquoted in his presence he could say at once, "That's not in the Bible," and he would help people with perfectly chosen quotations. He never carried out his project of translating the Latin Bible into Spanish, but he did write a book about the Apocalypse (the last book of the New Testament, written by St. John the Apostle), which after his death was published in Madrid.

Gergory never set himself up as "a master," or tried to instruct people unless he was asked; but in these later years clergy and lay people of all kinds came to consult this layman who had formerly been so despised. His advice and replies were always short and to the point: he deplored unnecessary talk, whether in himself or others—including his companion Don Losa, who was more than once quietly reproved for his talkativeness. Once in after years, when someone quoted the question of Eliphaz the Themanite (Job 4:2), "Who can withhold himself from speaking?" Don Losa retorted grimly, "Gregory Lopez could!"

Gregory used to say that "Some people talk a lot to God not out of love of Him but out of love of themselves. Love expresses itself in deeds: so let's not talk much—or at all."

"Perfection and merit," he used to say, "consist in our efforts to use all our powers in loving God in the most perfect way of which we are capable. If we do that, then we are loving God perfectly: that is the whole Law and the Prophets, and God asks nothing else from us." And when a priest asked him for a rule about prayer, Gregory—himself a man of intense prayer—simply reminded him of the prayer of Christ, "Our Father . . ."

Gregory was a tall, handsome man, with chestnut-colored hair and beard and a slightly sallow complexion; his eyes were black, "with green glints in them," and his thick curved eyebrows met. He was a little shortsighted but could always read without spectacles. The only things in his room besides necessities were a Bible, a map of the world, and a geographical globe. He made the last two himself. When some interfering person remarked sourly that there were no religious statues or holy pictures in the room, Gregory simply replied, "Don't worry. If you're scandalized, go to the 'higher-ups'— they'll know what to do." As well as a mapmaker he was a calligrapher; he could mend his own clothes and shoes, and made a hat last forever because he rarely wore it; and he knew something about anatomy as well as medicines. Certainly an all-round man.

Gregory Lopez was only fifty-four when he died, after two months of painful illness, on July 20, 1596. Many miracles were reported at his grave, relics of him were eagerly sought and, as I have already said, his memory came to be reverenced all over Mexico. But his fame spread further. His faithful friend Don Losa wrote his biography, and it was translated into English as early as 1675. But even before that it had been a favorite book of the Venerable Augustine Baker, a Welsh Benedictine monk who was one of the greatest spiritual writers the British Isles have ever produced. It is curious to think of a book about a Spanish layman in Mexico being treasured by a penal-times priest in England and on the continent.

10

APOSTLE OF CALIFORNIA

J UNIPER cannot be said to be a well-known Christian
name: it is more familiar as designating the genus of trees
and shrubs whose products are used in the making of such
diverse things as pencils, incense, and gin. But it is a popular
name among the Franciscan friars because of Brother Juniper,
one of St. Francis of Assisi's first companions, whom we read
about in *The Little Flowers of St. Francis;* and we may
expect that in the future it will become quite a popular name
in America, as Father Junípero Serra, the apostle of California, becomes more and more widely known.

At the beginning of the eighteenth century there were living on the island of Majorca, off the east coast of Spain, a
man in humble circumstances named Antonio Serra and his
wife Margaret Ferrer, and to them was born in 1713 a boy,
who was baptized Michael Joseph. His birthplace still stands
at Petra. He was a rather undersized lad, delicate in health,
but before he was seventeen he was accepted as a novice by
the Friars Minor of St. Francis at Palma, and when he made
his profession a year later he took the name of Junípero, for
he dearly loved to read the chronicles of the early days of his
order. As he grew older his health and his physique improved,
and he taught very successfully as a professor of philosophy,

but when he was thirty-five Father Junípero heard a call to preach the gospel to the heathen in the Indies. He arrived in Mexico in 1749, and his first assignment was to the missions in the Sierra Gorda Mountains, north of Querétaro.

His first experience here was disconcerting. There were about a thousand Indian converts, but not a single one came to confession and communion at Easter. It was the old trouble: the missionaries had insufficient knowledge of the Indians' language. Father Junípero at once set himself to learn it properly, and was then able to translate prayers for the Indians to learn by heart and instructions to be given to them. To induce them to come to confession he would—like St. Francis de Sales—set the example on great feasts, kneeling publicly at the feet of his confessor in front of the altar before Mass. Nor were his efforts confined to religion: he took an active interest in improving agriculture, extending trades, and finding markets, so that during Father Junípero's nine years in the Sierra Gorda, civilization kept pace with evangelization.

Then for nearly as long he was engaged in preaching and giving missions up and down Mexico, often in circumstances of the greatest hardship and danger. He traveled as much as possible on foot, in spite of a troublesome injury to one of his feet which was never cured; and he suited his methods to the sort of people with whom he had to deal, seeking to move them to penitence by such sensational means as scourging himself in public, beating his breast with a stone when in the pulpit, or applying fire to his bared flesh. His sermons seem sometimes to have been very long: after landing at Vera Cruz he preached at a thanksgiving service, giving, we are told, "a complete account of even the smallest circumstances and incidents of the long voyage of ninety-nine days" from Europe. Travelers are commonly apt to be talkative about their experiences; but no doubt this one used them to illustrate the goodness of God and His providential care.

Father Serra was fifty-five before he set foot in California. In 1767 King Charles III of Spain banished the Society of Jesus from his dominions, and the Jesuit missions in Lower California were handed over to the care of the Franciscans: sixteen friars were sent thither, with Father Junípero as their superior. He did not like having to exercise authority, and he was sorry to be once again going to missions that had been established by others; but very soon the Spanish inspector general was fitting out an expedition for Upper California, under Gaspar de Portolá, and Father Junípero was invited to join it. The plan was to establish missions for the first time at the harbors of San Diego and Monterey, with a third halfway between. That was to be the modest beginning of a great undertaking. At the last moment Father Francis Palou (who was to write the biography of Serra that we still have) tried to dissuade him from going, for his foot and leg were very bad; but Father Junípero would not be dissuaded, and at the end of June 1769 he crossed over into what is now the United States of America.

The expedition reached San Diego on July 1, and the prospect was a disheartening one. The seaborne part of the expedition had arrived, but all the crew of one of the two ships had died from scurvy, many others had sickened, and there were frequent raids by Indians. In one of these, on the feast of the Assumption, the friars' servant Joseph was shot in the throat by an arrow, and he died as he was given absolution. In such conditions did Father Junípero Serra found the first mission in what is now the state of California.

It was nearly a year later before Monterey was reached. Father Junípero tells us in a letter exactly how that occasion was celebrated:

> On the holy day of Pentecost, June 3, the military and naval officers and all the other people assembled at the side of the little ravine by the oak where the fathers of that other expedition [of Vizcaino] had held their celebration [in 1602]. An altar was made, bells hung up and chimed, *Veni Creator* was sung and water blessed, a large cross set up and the royal standard flown. I then sang the first Mass which, we supposed, had been celebrated here since that long time ago; and afterward we sang *Salve Regina* before the image of our most illustrious Queen on the altar. Then I preached to the assembly and the service ended with the *Te Deum*, after which the officers took formal possession of the land in the name of our lord the king (whom may God keep). Afterward we ate our dinner together in a shady spot on the beach. The whole service was accompanied by much thunder of powder both on land and from the ship. To God alone be all the honor and glory.

As at San Diego, the mission at Monterey (San Carlos) was subsequently moved farther away from the garrison, whose propinquity the friars found demoralizing for their converts.

The Indians of the coast as far north as Sonoma were evangelized and ministered to from twenty-one Franciscan missions between 1769 and 1834. They were by nature a more promising people than their fellows in Lower California, but tough enough material: the first conversion did not come for a year, and "In all the missionary annals of the northwest there is no other instance where paganism remained stubborn so long" (H. H. Bancroft, *History of California*). The nine of these missions founded by Serra himself were San Diego (St. Didacus), San Carlos (St. Charles Borromeo), San Antonio (St. Anthony of Padua), San Gabriel (the Archangel),[1] San Luis Obispo (St. Louis the Bishop, *i.e.*, Louis of Toulouse), San Francisco (St. Francis of Assisi), San Juan Capistrano (St. John of Capistrano), Santa Clara (St. Clare), and San Buenaventura (St. Bonaventure; now "Ventura").

What is perhaps the best known of all the Franciscan missions, Santa Barbara, was not established as a mission till two years after Serra's death, but he was present at its foundation as a military station in 1782. He was unable to locate a mission there then because of difficulties with the provincial governor. The Holy See had granted Father Junípero the privilege of giving the sacrament of confirmation, and the governor, by his insistence on departmental "red tape," had prevented him from exercising this right for nearly two years —that is the sort of thing that happens when there is too close an association between church and state.[2] Nor was this the only time that Serra's work was hampered by the civil power: some years before he had trouble with the military authorities, and had had to make the long, toilsome journey to the viceroy in Mexico City to get it straightened out.

Father Junípero labored in Upper California for fifteen years, and "labored" is the word. It is recorded that he con-

[1] Within the bounds of this mission was formed the settlement of Nuestra Señora de los Angeles de la Porciuncula, named for the church of Our Lady of the Angels "of the Little Piece," near Assisi. It is now the city of Los Angeles.

[2] It was not so common then as it is now for missionary priests and others in certain circumstances to be allowed to give confirmation.

firmed 5,309 persons, nearly all of them Indians converted by himself and his fellow Franciscans. This is a figure that carries more conviction than such figures sometimes do. During his last three years he revisited all the missions from San Diego to San Francisco, in spite of increasing suffering from his bad foot and a weakness in the chest. At San Carlos on August 18, 1784, Father Palou noticed and commented on the vigor of his singing. "We mustn't be too sure," replied a soldier. "This holy father is always well when it is a matter of praying and singing. But he is nearly finished." And he was right. Ten days later Junípero Serra was dead. After feeling unwell for some days, he received viaticum publicly in the church, and then retired to his adobe cell for the last anointing. Next morning two naval officers visited him and talked about their voyage to Peru. "Well, gentlemen," said Father Junípero, "it is a long time since we met last and you have been a long way. I'm glad you have been able to come so far as this, in time to throw a little earth on my body." The officers were astonished, for he seemed pretty well; but at two o'clock that afternoon, as he lay quietly and alone upon his bed, God called him to the better life.

Father Junípero Serra was not simply a great missionary of the Americas: he is among the outstanding missionaries of the world. His qualities were those of all great missionaries—whether in a heroic degree the Holy See will tell us in due course—and his "secret" was theirs; love of the people for whose sake he left father and mother and kindred to preach the good news of Christ. He more than once told the civil authorities that should the Indians ever kill him his murderers were not to be punished. He used to refer to his work as "this spiritual conquest": a warfare of which the end was not *Vae victis,* "Woe to the defeated," but happiness, eternal happiness, to those in whom heathenism was overcome. "We might say of him," wrote Father Palou, "what Pliny said of the tree whose name he bears, that 'The juniper is a tree that flourishes in waste places: snakes avoid its shade, so that in that shade men rest in safety.'"

No other missionary in the Americas is honored by so many public monuments. It is sufficient to name one, the first, on Presidio Hill overlooking the bay of Monterey, due to the *pietas* and generosity of a Protestant lady, Mrs. Jane Leland Stanford. But the most moving is necessarily the simple grave in the San Carlos Church at Carmel, with its brief and sufficient inscription: "IHS. Fr. JUNÍPERO SERRA, Apostol de California, 1713-1784." We may look forward confidently to great pilgrimages to that grave in time to come, for the documents of information in the cause of the beatification of Father Junípero Serra were carried from the Bishop of Monterey-Fresno to Rome in 1950.

11

THE SLAVE OF THE NEGROES

T HE honor of having begun the work of abolishing the slave trade belongs to England, and will ever be connected with the names of H. W. Wilberforce and David Livingstone. Another worker in the cause, Cardinal Lavigerie, Archbishop of Algiers, visiting the grave of the Protestant Livingstone in London, said to those around him, "Gentlemen, you are the heirs of his glory, and you must carry out his wishes." The other side of the picture is that England, in the persons of such national figures as Sir John Hawkins, played a considerable part in establishing that trade between Africa and the New World in the sixteenth century. And if there were also many Catholics who carried on that wicked trade, there were as well some who devoted their lives to helping its victims, the Negroes. Among them, none was greater than St. Peter Claver.

He was born in Spain in 1581, the son of a farmer, and when he was twenty joined the Society of Jesus. Having been inspired by the lay brother St. Alphonsus Rodriguez to offer himself for the American missions, he was sent to the Jesuit house at Santa Fé de Bogotá to complete his studies, and in

1615 he was ordained priest at Cartagena, in what is now the republic of Colombia.

By this time the slave trade had been established with South America for nearly a hundred years, and the port of Cartagena was one of its chief centers. Negroes were bought in West Africa for four crowns a head, or exchanged for goods, and sold in America for 200 crowns. The conditions in which they were conveyed across the Atlantic were so frightful that the standard rate of loss by death during the six or seven weeks' voyage was fifty per cent of each cargo; yet in spite of that an average of ten thousand living slaves was landed at Cartagena every year.

Condemnation of this great crime by Pope Paul III and by other churchmen had no effect; the most the owners did was to have their slaves baptized. But they received no religious instruction or ministrations, nothing was done to improve their lot, and so the sacrament of baptism became to the Negroes the very sign and symbol of their oppression. The clergy did what little they could, but felt paralyzed in the face of such a huge problem. And then along came Father Claver, proclaiming that "I am the slave of the Negroes forever."

From the start he thoroughly organized the work. He enlisted bands of helpers, whether by money, goods, or services, and when a slave ship came in he hurried down to the freight yards. There were hundreds of men who for weeks had been packed like hogs in the ship's hold now all herded together—well, ill, or dying—in a confined space in a hot, humid climate. The scene was revolting and physically almost unbearable. Into these yards and sheds Peter Claver plunged, with medicines and food, bread, brandy, lemons, tobacco. "We must speak to them with our hands before we try to speak to them with our lips," he would say, echoing the words of St. Thomas Aquinas, "A hungry man must be fed, not instructed."

It must be admitted that most of the clergy had made little effort to master the Negroes' language in order that they might instruct them. Father Claver enlisted a group of interpreters to help him, but even so found it very difficult sometimes to make himself understood. So he made use of pictures as well: for example, of our Lord suffering on the cross, and of popes, kings, and other great men among the Whites standing by and rejoicing at the baptism of a colored man. One of his most critical and one of his hardest tasks was to try to teach them some little self-respect. He had never heard of "modern psychology," but he knew that a feeling of inferiority is one of the most difficult things to get by, for it can prevent people from feeling shame at their own misdeeds and from understanding that they can do better, and that God cares for them even if nobody else seems to. The slaves were treated as the scum of the earth, and so they learned to think that that was just what they were. It gives us some faint idea of Father Claver's difficulties that they were very slow even in learning how to make the sign of the cross, and at baptism each group of them was given the *same* Christian name, so that they could help one another to remember it.

And yet, it is estimated, in forty years St. Peter Claver instructed and baptized 300,000 Negroes and he is said to have heard the confessions of more than five thousand in one year.

When the slaves were sent off to the mines and plantations, they passed out of Father Claver's sphere of action. He could then but pray for them and do all he could to soften the hearts and influence the minds of their masters. That was a hardly less difficult job. But at least it must be said for the Spaniards that the worst of them seem to have been better than some of the English slaveowners in the seventeenth and eighteenth centuries, in Jamaica, for example. The laws of Spain at least provided for slaves to get married, forbade the breaking up of families, and would not allow re-enslavement after liberation. Of course these laws were very often broken, and Father Claver did all he could to get them enforced.

As is always the way with Christian reformers, some of his greatest opposition came from people who professed to be Christians. Planters complained that he wasted the slaves' time with his preaching and praying and singing; their wives wrinkled their delicate noses and said that the atmosphere of a church after the slaves had been to Mass was more than they could put up with. They got even some of the bishops on their side, and poor Father Claver groaned, "What sort of a man am I that I can't do a little good without causing all this trouble?"

That modest remark is very characteristic of Father Claver's humility, which was anything but the copybook kind. He once said that he was not really zealous and apostolic at all, that his work was actually a sort of self-indulgence, because it ministers to "my enthusiastic and impulsive temperament. If I hadn't something like this to do I should get into mischief and be a nuisance to people." And the loathsome physical conditions in which so much of his work was carried out drew

from him the observation, "I can't taste and I've got a strong stomach. If that makes a saint, then maybe I am one."

St. Peter Claver realized that any real and permanent improvement in the spiritual and material conditions of the Negroes depended in great measure on raising the standard of Christianity among the people in general. So he became not only the apostle of the slaves but the apostle of Cartagena as well. The work he got through was enormous. He sometimes had to spend fifteen hours in the confessional at a stretch, and yet found time to minister on the scaffold to every man condemned to death—and they were numerous. Every spring he gave a round of missions among the planters; every fall the same among the seamen and traders of the port. Sometimes he would spend a day preaching in public in the main square of the city; at other times he would be working in the hospitals. He tried to convert Mohammedan sailors off the merchant ships, but had very little success (nobody has); similar work among Protestant seamen from England bore more fruit, and he was able, on one occasion, to reconcile an Anglican clergyman with the Church. It is not surprising that his very name became a power. It is said that on one occasion a man got rid of a loose woman who was pestering him in the street by saying, "Look out! Here comes Father Claver!"

The year 1650 was a holy year, and Peter Claver was sent to preach a jubilee mission to the Negroes along the coast. Here he contracted a disease—perhaps a sort of malaria—that practically incapacitated him for the rest of his life. We may imagine what a trial that was to the patience of so vigorous a man. But there was even worse. For a long time he was left in the care of a young Negro, who took no care at all. He was rough and impatient with the old man (he was now seventy), and sometimes left him lying helpless in bed for days on end. To put it bluntly, Father Claver was neglected and forgotten. "Ah well," he said, "I must be God's pack mule."

But God was not going to let his servant die like this. In the summer of 1654 came the good news that Father Diego de Fariña had been sent from Spain to devote himself to the Negroes. Father Claver dragged himself from bed to welcome him, and to give him the fruits of all his rich experience. Then he waited for the end. For the last time he heard the confession of his good friend and benefactress of the Negroes, Doña Isabella de Urbina. On September 6 he received holy communion—he knew that this was his viaticum, but nobody else did. That very evening he was taken ill, and fell into a stupor from which he never fully recovered. On the birthday of our Lady, September 8, 1654, St. Peter Claver died.

From that moment he was suddenly remembered again, never afterward to be forgotten. He was given a public funeral, with all those civil honors for which he did not care a bit. What would have warmed his heart was that the Negroes and the Indians arranged a solemn Mass of requiem on their own, at which a high ecclesiastic preached and the Spanish authorities were present. Two hundred and thirty-four years later he was canonized, at the same time as his friend St. Alphonsus Rodriguez, and in 1896 Pope Leo XIII declared him patron of all missionary work for Negroes throughout the world.

We have seen in our age crimes so frightful and states of mind so corrupt that we are apt to believe some of them cannot be paralleled in the history of the world. That may be so, or it may not. We have the best of reasons for knowing, at any rate, that the heart of man has always been "desperately wicked." But it is worth noticing that among the charges brought against St. Peter Claver by people who proclaimed themselves Catholic Christians was that he "profaned the sacraments by giving them to creatures who hardly possessed a soul"; i.e., Negroes. The man who did this thing was canonized; the people who spoke and thought in that way are remembered only with shame.

12

AN OAK IN THE
WILDERNESS

୧◊୨

T HOSE who like to look for meanings and prophecies in
people's names can find a good example in that of the
second woman to be beatified in the United States of America: Rose Philippine Duchesne. She was called Rose at baptism because she was born in France in 1769 on the eve of the
feast of St. Rose of Lima, the first canonized saint of the
Americas. And her surname summed up an outstanding quality in her character, *du chesne*, "of the oak."

That quality, that character, can be seen throughout the
life of Blessed Philippine (as she is usually called). She never
found it easy to bend her own will to the orders of her superiors or to the will of God. It was a characteristic inherited
from her father's family; the Duchesnes were known in Gren-
oble as "stiff" people. Imperious and stubborn—*entêté* is the
French word, with its suggestion of "headstrong": they meant
to have their own way, or to know the reason why not. That
was Rose Duchesne all over: "a strong and very impetuous
character," as the first and best of her biographers, Monsignor
Baunard, calls her.

But although her character was plain enough from the start,

and her future therefore more than usually unpredictable, there was little in Philippine's early life to suggest how and where it would end. She was nearly fifty before she set foot in the New World. But the smallest thing may be important in an individual's life, and there was one small thing in her very early days. When Philippine was eight, a Jesuit father visited her home; he had been a missionary in the huge Louisiana of those days, and he talked about his experiences. That awakened her interest in America, and especially the Indians. Philippine never forgot those Indians.

The Duchesnes were wealthy business people, and they gave their daughter a good education, by which she was well able to profit. By the time she was seventeen she was in every way an attractive young woman, and her parents set about finding a good husband for her. When, therefore, she declared she was going to be a nun, there was domestic consternation and some trouble. However, her father gave in, and Philippine joined the convent of Visitation nuns at Ste. Marie-d'en-Haut where she had been at school. But she was not destined to make her profession with them. At the French Revolution the nuns were expelled from their house, and Sister Philippine had to go back to her family. For ten years she had to live as best she could as a nun "in the world." She looked after her folks, taught children, nursed the sick, succored the victims of the Revolution. Then, when better times came, she tried to re-establish the Visitation convent at Ste. Marie-d'en-Haut. The attempt was an utter failure.

And so, in 1804, with the encouragement of an old friend who was a priest, Sister Philippine offered herself and the buildings to Mother Barat, who had recently founded the first convent of the Society of the Sacred Heart at Amiens. Both were accepted; and thus were brought together St. Madeleine Sophie Barat and Blessed Philippine Duchesne: two souls, says Monsignor Baunard, of whom the one was marble and the other bronze, or, as it might be paraphrased, teak and oak. In the years that followed, these two strong souls developed a great respect for each other, a friendship that neither the Atlantic nor death itself could sever.

Mother Duchesne had been professed only a few months when something happened to bring America vividly to her mind again. This was a visit to Ste. Marie-d'en-Haut of Abbot Augustine de Lestrange, who had a few years before sent to the United States its first Cistercian ("Trappist") monks, whose wonderful diffusion throughout the Union we ourselves are seeing today. All her old longing to give herself to the service of what was then a vast missionary territory came back with redoubled force, and she offered herself as a volunteer. "Fine!" said Mother Barat in effect. "But I am not sending any Sacred Heart religious to America. Go on with your work here, dear mother."

And so she did, for another twelve years. "She teaches in school all day, sits up at night with the sick children, does the whole outside management of the house," wrote St. Madeleine Sophie, "and yet she never shows distress, and hardly seems to be overworked. What a woman!" It was certainly good training for one who wanted to go to early nineteenth-century America; but that Duchesne character was still strong—both ways. Philippine talked so much about America and the foreign missions that at last Mother Barat had to forbid her to refer to the subject. And when she was given an important office in the Sacred Heart Society and sent to its mother house in Paris, America seemed farther away than ever. Then there came another visitor. This time it was a bishop, Louis Dubourg, of Louisiana. He wanted some Sacred Heart nuns for his diocese. Mother Barat said he should have them, and the bishop went away delighted. But Mother Barat did not act at once; and he might never have gotten his nuns but for the energy of Mother Duchesne, who at last saw her chance of serving God in the way she was convinced He wanted. In March 1818 she sailed from Bordeaux, with Mother Berthold, Mother André, and two lay sisters. Like Mother Cabrini (who would not be born for another thirty-two years), Philippine Duchesne did not like the sea, and the voyage was rough. "Seasickness is really bad," she wrote later. "It upsets the head as well as the stomach, and makes one quite useless." She had hoped to utilize the long voyage in studying the English language; again like Mother Cabrini, she found it very difficult, and indeed never mastered it properly.

The day of their landing at New Orleans, May 29, was a propitious one, for it was the feast of the Sacred Heart that year. After a rest they went on up the Mississippi, and found Bishop Dubourg at Saint Louis, which in those days was no more than a large village of a few thousand inhabitants, in a wilderness given over to rangers and Indians. The bishop installed them at the Saint Charles settlement, to the north-west of Saint Louis. Their convent was a log cabin.

Here Mother Duchesne and her companions started the first free school to be opened west of the Mississippi. But the winter was very hard; Mother Duchesne suffered in health,

and by the end of the next year Bishop Dubourg had moved the nuns to a brick building at Florisant, nearer to Saint Louis. It was not good management to time the move for the depths of winter. They had a fearsome trek, in the course of which their cow broke loose and had to be recaptured by Mother Duchesne.

The white population of the district was predominantly French in origin and therefore mostly Catholic, but extreme ignorance, both religious and other, and frontier toughness prevailed. Mother Duchesne remarked that many of their pupils were well supplied with gowns, while their underclothes were insufficient and pocket handkerchiefs nonexistent. As for the Indians, "We used to have pleasant dreams of teaching docile and innocent savages; but the women are lazy, and drink as much as the men."

There is no doubt that Blessed Philippine came to America with only the haziest ideas of what it was really like; she found the reality puzzling and often unpleasant. She was now middle-aged, with her ideas and ways formed, and fixed, moreover, in a strongly European mold. It is not surprising that she was baffled both by the virtues and the faults of frontier Americans, and that she probably never came to be at ease and wholly tactful in dealing with them. But her spirit was not daunted—she heard there were Indians in Peru and wanted to set off at once to convert them. "However," she wrote to Mother Barat, "I am more reasonable now than when I used to pester you in France with my wild schemes."

Very soon Mother Duchesne had to make a long trip down-river for a second foundation at Grand Coteau, 150 miles from New Orleans. It took a month and was no picnic; but it was child's play compared to the return journey, which took nearly twice as long. It was begun on a boat that had yellow fever aboard. The sick were shunned and left unattended by the rest, who feared for themselves; and in this nightmare of suffering and selfishness Blessed Philippine did what she could to relieve and help the neglected. In particular she cared for one stricken man, who asked for and received baptism from her before he died. Then she herself fell sick and was put ashore at Natchez, where there was no place for her to go except to the bed of a woman who had herself just been carried off by the fever. Philippine had many difficult journeys, but never another so bad as that: it nearly cost her life.

But had she been able to see the future she would have borne it even more willingly, for a fruit of the foundation at Grand Coteau was of the greatest importance to the Society of the Sacred Heart. One of its first pupils was Mary Aloysia Hardey, who between 1841 and 1883 was to establish a score of convents in the Eastern states and extend the Society to Canada and Cuba.

The beginnings of the establishment at Florisant were sufficiently encouraging to start a novitiate there, and soon the first American member received the habit of the society: her name, Mary Layton; the date, November 22, 1820. But this good beginning did not last. There were a boarding and day school for fee-paying pupils, as well as the free school, but the nuns found it difficult to meet their expenses; they often did not have enough to eat. Things were made very much worse by the jealousy, ingratitude, misunderstandings, and calumnies of outsiders. "People say everything bad they can about us, except that we poison the children," wrote Mother Duchesne, and parents took their children away from a school so evilly spoken of. But she put on a brave front and refused to give in, even when the pupils were reduced to five.

Help came unexpectedly in 1823. The Jesuits of Maryland moved their novitiate to Florisant, and thenceforward the nuns had the support and encouragement of the fathers, and the fathers had the assistance of the nuns. Within five years the school at Saint Charles had been reopened and three others were established, at Saint Michaels near New Orleans, at Bayou-la-Fourche, and at Saint Louis itself. The private school for Catholic girls and the free school were the first of their kind to be opened in that city.

St. Madeleine Sophie Barat was right when she said that God himself had entrusted to Blessed Philippine this mission in a land where, in Philippine's own words, "there is want, but also Christian heroism, where the only wealth of the clergy is their trials." Every succeeding year brought its troubles, disappointments, and hardships, not the least of which was ill health that tried Philippine's endurance to the utmost. But now only the good side of the Duchesne character was in evidence: mellowness came with advancing age, austerity and sternness were sweetened by affliction.

In 1840 Mother Barat sent her assistant general to make a visitation of the American houses of the society. This religious, Mother Elizabeth Gallitzin, belonged to one of the most illustrious of Russian houses, the family that gave to the Church Father Dmitry Gallitzin ("Mr. Augustine Smith"), the heroic apostle of the country around Loretto, Pennsylvania. Mother Gallitzin was burning with zeal and enthusiasm, but her nature was stern, imperious, and autocratic—she was, in fact, not unlike Mother Duchesne in earlier times. These two now faced each other: Mother Gallitzin, vigorous in the prime of life (she was forty-three), with a wholly European background; Blessed Philippine, twenty-eight years older, worn out with the hard experience of twenty years as a missionary in the Mississippi Valley.

It was only to be expected that Mother Gallitzin's methods and temperament should provoke disturbance among the American nuns. Blessed Philippine was patient and did not resist her, for she came with the authority of the mother general. But the sad thing was that Philippine was given the impression that she herself had failed in her mission—she who had labored all those years and successfully planted the Society of the Sacred Heart in America, cut off all the time from the counsel and experience of St. Madeleine Sophie, except through the medium of a slow and uncertain mail. So she asked to be allowed to resign her office as superior. Mother Gallitzin accepted the proposal with enthusiasm.

And so the pioneer who had blazed the trail along which others advanced to spread the Society of the Sacred Heart over the New World retired to the Saint Louis convent as a simple religious. But it was not a retirement yet. Blessed Philippine was old—seventy-one—tired out with responsibility, work, and ill health. But when the Jesuit Father de Smet asked Mother Gallitzin for some nuns to work among the Potawatomi Indians in Kansas, Mother Duchesne was given permission to be one of them, "if she were able to travel." Mother Duchesne was always able to travel when the good of others required it.

More than sixty years after she had first heard tales of the American Indians, Blessed Philippine went with three other sisters to set up a school in the Potawatomi mission at Sugar Creek. It would perhaps have been kinder had superiors not let her go. It was not that she became disillusioned about the "docile and innocent savages"—that had happened twenty years before at Saint Charles. She was just too old and too weary; the life was too hard, she could not master the Potawatomi language. And yet this indomitable old nun was not daunted: she wanted to press on farther west, to the Rockies—

there were Indians there who had never heard the name of Christ.

It was soon decided that Mother Duchesne had to be withdrawn from an assignment that was clearly too much for her. "I don't know why they are fetching me back," she said, "but God knows, and that is enough."

Blessed Philippine spent her last ten years where her American life had begun, at Saint Charles, Missouri. A religious of the time said of her, "She was the St. Francis of Assisi of the Society of the Sacred Heart. Everything about her was stamped with the seal of a crucified life. She would have liked to disappear from the sight of men, and it may indeed be said that no one occupied less space in the world than Madame Duchesne. Her room was a miserable hole with a single window in which paper took the place of some of the panes; her bed was a mattress two inches thick, laid on the ground by night and put away in a cupboard by day; her only covering at night was an old piece of black stuff with a cross on it like a pall."

But even those closing years cannot be pictured simply as a holy and mortified retirement in which Blessed Philippine peacefully watched the even progress of the work she had begun. It did not progress in that way at all. The Society of the Sacred Heart still had to suffer setbacks in America. Convents that Philippine had founded and nursed were threatened with dissolution; and though she saw the establishment of the first Sacred Heart convent in the Eastern states (by Mother Hardey and Mother Gallitzin in New York), she also saw the closing of the one at Florisant. So Blessed Philippine suffered to the end, which came so far as this world is concerned on November 18, 1852. Already those who knew her best spoke of a possible canonization: eighty-eight years later the first stage was achieved with her beatification by Pope Pius XII.

13
INTERRACIAL PATRON

AMONG the people to whom the epithet "half-caste" is often given as a term of contempt, the first of whom it is recorded that he displayed Christian virtue in a heroic degree was a Dominican lay brother in Peru; and it is fitting that in recent years interest in and devotion to him should have spread so widely in the United States, where the slavery of the past has left so painful a legacy of social problems.

Martin de Porres was born in Lima in 1579, the illegitimate child of John de Porres (Porras), a Spanish knight, and a colored freed woman from Panama, Anna by baptism. Young Martin inherited the features and dark complexion of his mother, which was a matter of vexation to the noble Porres, who at first refused to acknowledge the boy and his sister as his children. After a time he did so, however, but eventually left Martin to the care of his mother, and when he was twelve she apprenticed him to a barber surgeon. Thus the boy got an opportunity to learn something about medicine and pharmacy, and he began seriously to concern himself with the needs of the poor both in body and soul. Love of God grew hand in hand with love of his neighbor, and after three years, having received the habit of the third order of St. Dominic, Martin was admitted to the Rosary convent of the Friars

Preachers at Lima, where he eventually became a professed lay brother.

"Many were the offices to which the servant of God, Brother Martin de Porres, attended, being barber, surgeon, wardrobe keeper, and infirmarian. Each of these jobs was enough for one man, but alone he filled them all with great liberality, promptness, and carefulness, without being weighed down by any of them. It was most striking, and it made me [Brother Fernando de Aragones] realize that, in that he clung to God in his soul, all these things were effects of divine grace." No work was too lowly for Martin to do with care and interest: he did not understand the meaning of the word "drudgery." Once, when he was cleaning out the washrooms, a friar said to him jokingly, "Well, Brother Martin, don't you think you'd be better off in the archbishop's mansion rather than doing this job here?" To which Martin replied with a quotation from the 83rd psalm. "I would rather," he said, "be a doorkeeper in the house of God than a guest in the tents of the wicked." By which, of course, he did not mean any disrespect to the archbishop—whom he respected and who respected him—but simply that he preferred to be a mendicant friar for the love of God rather than in what the world would regard as a more exalted position.

Humility sometimes provokes insult. On one occasion a fellow friar rounded on Martin and called him—unbelievable as it may seem—"a dog of a mulatto, no better than a galley slave." The description was accepted without demur. And when his priory was being dunned for a debt, Martin offered himself in payment: "I am only a poor mulatto; I'm the property of the order: sell me." But it was another mat-

ter when Brother Cyprian de Medina was taunted by some
graceless fellow novices for his clumsiness and unattractive
face. Martin would not stand for that. "You call Brother
Cyprian ugly," he told them. "All right. But remember this:
he will grow into a fine young man and be a credit to the
order." And so it was: Cyprian lived to be a bishop and to
testify to Brother Martin's holiness for the process of beatification.

Blessed Martin extended his care of the sick to those of the
city, and the poor thronged the gates of the friary. All of
them, Spaniards, Indians, the miserable Negro slaves from
Africa, were received with the same consideration and care.
But the time came when these poor folk began to be found in
all sorts of irregular places, and the prior provincial had to
forbid him to bring any more sick beggars into the friary,
whether to lodge them in his own cell or anywhere else. So
Martin invoked for them the shelter of his sister's house; and
through his influence with a wealthy merchant he was instru-
mental in establishing an orphanage and foundling hospital,
with other charitable institutions attached, which under the
name of Holy Cross did great good in Peru. But his physick-
ing speaks to us of another age; one of his remedies was
boiled toad, ground to powder and worn in a bag around the
waist.

Martin was very desirous of going to some foreign mission
where he might earn the crown of martyrdom, but as this was
impossible he made a martyr of his own body. Those who
knew him say much about his severe penances; much, too,
about his ecstasies at prayer, levitations, and other supernatural gifts. The priory's daily alms of food to the hungry is

said sometimes to have been increased miraculously when he
distributed it, and that is far from being the only miracle
attributed to him. Many were concerned with the healing of
the sick; others involved those strange phenomena, such as
"bilocation," into a consideration of which we ordinary folk
are well advised not to venture without a trusty guide.

The love and charity of Blessed Martin embraced the
lower animals (which seems to have surprised the Spaniards)
and even vermin, excusing the depredations of rats and mice
on the ground that the poor little things were insufficiently
fed. He had a good word even for mosquitoes, and he kept
a "cats' and dogs' home" at his sister's house. (We should
like to know more about Joan de Porres.) It is in connection
with animals that we are given a glimpse of Martin "at recre-
ation." He spent a lot of time working at the friars' farm in
the country, and here he used to play at bullfights with the
calves, using his Dominican *cappa* as a *chulo's* cloak: the calves
enjoyed it as much as he did. (We may be sure that this is
as near a bullfight as Blessed Martin ever got; it was only a
few years before he was born that Pope St. Pius V—likewise
a Dominican—sternly condemned what Cardinal Gasparri
called in our own time "these bloodthirsty and shameful
spectacles.") The same witness, John Vasquez Parra, whom
Martin had picked out of the gutter, shows the lay brother
as eminently practical in his charities, using carefully and
methodically the money and goods he collected, raising a
dowry for his niece in three days (at the same time getting as
much and more for the poor), putting up the banns, showing
Vasquez how to sow camomile in the well-manured hoof-
prints of cattle, buying a Negro servant to work in the

laundry, looking after those who needed blankets, shirts, candles, candies, miracles, or prayers—the procurator, apparently, both of the priory and of the public.

Don Balthasar Carasco, a jurist, wanted to be Brother Martin's "adopted son" and to call him "father," such was his admiration for him. Martin objected: "Why do you want a mulatto for a father? That would not look well." "Why not? It would rather be said that you have a Spaniard for a son," retorted Don Balthasar. This same lawyer deposed that, "I often consulted him about my family troubles, those disputes that arise between husband and wife. Several times, as I was going to him about such things, he came out to meet me and talked with me about my troubles before I had told him what they were, and gave me good advice. . . ." In the same way Martin was able to forestall the wreck of his own sister's married life: the couple found that he seemed to know more about their difficulties than they did themselves. They listened to his wisdom and accepted his reproofs; and they were reconciled.

St. Rose of Lima was a close friend of Blessed Martin, and so was Blessed John Massias, who was a lay brother at the Dominican priory of St. Mary Magdalen in the same town. Martin died at the Rosary priory on November 3, 1639, in his sixtieth year. He was carried to his grave by prelates and noblemen. Very soon the process of his beatification was begun, but there were long delays and setbacks, and it was not till 1837 that it was achieved. A century later began the remarkable diffusion of his veneration outside his native land which has led to such a widespread hope for his early canonization.

14

MOTHER SETON

❦

BOTH the Venerable Mary of the Incarnation and Elizabeth Ann Seton were married women who after some
years of widowhood "in the world" became nuns; but there
the external resemblance ends, for little could be more dis-
similar than their respective backgrounds and early experiences and the circumstances of their religious life. Mary Martin
was, as we have seen, a French *petite bourgeoise*, who established the Ursulines in seventeenth-century Quebec; Mother
Seton was an American, raised an Episcopalian in the high
New York society of a century later, who founded the Sisters
of Charity in the United States.

Near the famous shrine of Our Lady of Walsingham in
England is the ancient town of King's Lynn; and from there,
about the year 1740, a young man called Bayley came to
America and married Miss Lecomte, of a family of Huguenot
descent in New Rochelle, New York. One of their sons,
Richard, became the first professor of anatomy in Columbia
University, and he married the daughter of an Episcopalian
clergyman of Staten Island, Catherine Charlton. They had
three daughters, the second of whom, Elizabeth Ann, was
born in New York City on August 28, 1774.[1] When she was

---

1 Her mother died three years later. Dr. Bayley married again, into the family that
gave its name to Barclay Street in New York, and a grandson of this marriage, James
Roosevelt Bayley, became the eighth archbishop of Baltimore.

nine years old she saw the redcoats marching out of New York and the Stars and Stripes hoisted over the city.

Elizabeth Bayley was a beautiful girl in soul and body. Her devoted father brought her up with great care and kindness, and to a considerable extent educated her himself. He was, it seems, something of a "free thinker," and Voltaire and Rousseau were part of his daughter's reading. But the stepmother, an Episcopalian, was a devout woman, and it was from her earliest years that Elizabeth learned the love and knowledge of the Bible and of such books as the *Imitation of Christ* which were never to leave her. In 1794, when she was not yet quite twenty, Elizabeth married William Seton, son of a wealthy Scottish merchant who kept "the most agreeable house in New York"; and fifteen months later their first child was born at their home, No. 27 Wall Street, which was then a very different neighborhood from what it is today.

The earlier years of Elizabeth's married life were serene and happy. Other children were born, and she formed a close friendship with her sister-in-law Rebecca; together they went about on errands of mercy, earning the prophetic nickname of "Protestant Sisters of Charity." But after the death of Mr. Seton, senior, and of Dr. Bayley, business worries and bad health began to tell on her husband, and it was decided to make a trip to Italy. It had the opposite result to what was hoped: because of yellow fever they were long detained in quarantine at Leghorn, and during the last days of 1803 William Seton died, at Pisa. In her distress and difficulty Elizabeth was generously befriended by Italian friends of her husband, the Filicchi, one of whom, Antonio, eventually accompanied her back to America. It was now that she made her first contacts with Catholicity, visiting churches in Italy and seeing it in action in the ungrudging kindness of her friends.

Within a few weeks of her return to New York her beloved Rebecca Seton, "the friend of her soul," was dead, and a time of spiritual turmoil and perplexity began for Elizabeth. She was torn between desire to become a Catholic and affection and respect for her friends and relations and all the ties of the life in which she had been brought up. On the one side Philip Filicchi, brother of Antonio, urged her to instant action; on the other, Mr. Hobart, whom she greatly respected, ably urged the claims of the Episcopal Church of which he was a minister. She was invited to join the Presbyterians, the Baptists, the Society of Friends. Elizabeth fasted and prayed. "If I am right, thy grace impart still in the right to stay. If I am wrong, Oh! teach my heart to find a better way." Bishop Carroll himself was drawn into the discussion; and a letter from him to Mr. Filicchi, together with one to Elizabeth from Father John Cheverus (afterwards first bishop of Boston and later a cardinal), seems to have been decisive. On March 14, 1805, Elizabeth Seton was received into the Catholic Church by Father Matthew O'Brien, o.p., in the old St. Peter's church on Barclay Street.

Mrs. Seton had found peace of soul; but peace of life was not yet to be hers. The conversion to "popery" of a member of families prominent in New York society was not an everyday occurrence, and Protestants were honestly outraged in their religious susceptibilities. Most of her friends—and friendship meant a lot to Elizabeth—deserted her; Mrs. Dupleix, Mrs. Sadler, and Mrs. Scott alone were faithful.

Because of the opposition of her relatives, she had to find a way to support herself and her five children. So she joined a Catholic man and his wife who had started a school for boys. But people were persuaded that the school was simply a proselytizing institution, and soon it had to close. Then it was arranged for Elizabeth to take charge of a boarding house for boys attached to a school in the Bowery. But the conversion of her sister-in-law Cecilia just at this time stirred up more trouble: there were threats to get Elizabeth expelled from the state as a dangerous person, and she had to give up the boarding house. Once again she was dependent on the tireless charity of the Filicchi, who even offered her a home in Italy. Happily for America, she was persuaded not to accept it.

In 1808, with the help of the Sulpician Fathers of St. Mary's College, Elizabeth Seton and her children removed to Baltimore and there opened a school for girls. She wrote to Antonio Filicchi, "If I ever dared ask God for anything touching our temporal future it would most assuredly be that we might never be forced to return to New York." She never was. The school prospered; but Elizabeth was anxious to devote herself to the children of the poor with a religious community, and "out of the blue" a gentleman from Virginia, Samuel Cooper, bought a farm at the village of Emmitsburg in Maryland for that purpose. Already a small band of young women had gathered around her in Baltimore; to these Bishop Carroll gave permission to wear a religious habit and to install themselves at Emmitsburg. The journey was made by covered wagon, and Mrs. Seton and her community took possession of the Fleming farm, afterward known as the Stone House. It was July 30, 1809; Elizabeth was thirty-five years old, and her children also were present.

The early days of the Emmitsburg community were full of hardship and privation, fully in the tradition of American pioneers. During the war with England in 1812–14 and at other times its existence was seriously threatened by the pressure of poverty. But aspirants were not wanting, and after the new house which Mr. Cooper provided was occupied and a boarding and day school opened, there were increasing numbers of applications from would-be postulants. The spirit of the community was shown by one of its younger members who, in the middle of a discussion of their difficulties, exclaimed, "My dear sisters, don't grieve so much. Depend upon it, this valley, quiet as it is, will one day give such a roar that all America will hear it. Don't you remember what was said about the silence of St. Thomas Aquinas?"

It had been decided to adopt the rule of the Sisters of Charity, founded by St. Vincent de Paul and St. Louise de Marillac, and arrangements were made for three sisters to come over from France to train the new community; but to spite the Sulpicians, Napoleon Bonaparte refused to let them go.[2] That was the rule adopted, however, and in 1813 Mother Seton and eighteen others made their vows. It is from that humble company that the great diffusion and endless good work of the Sisters of Charity in the United States today have sprung.

Mother Seton was a highly cultivated woman. Among the enthusiasms of her youth were Milton and James Thomson;

2 The superior of Saint-Sulpice, M. Emery, had stood up to Napoleon over his treatment of Pope Pius VII.

in later years it was the French spiritual writers, from whose
works she made translations. Many volumes of her own dia-
ries and letters are still in existence, and some of them have
been published. She was associated with some of the most
famous clergy of a decisive period in American Catholic history—Carroll, Cheverus, Dubourg, Dubois, Flaget, Bruté—
and she had boundless respect for the priesthood. Careless
preaching shocked her. To a young priest who admitted taking little trouble in preparing a sermon she said, "Sir, that
awakens my anger. Do you remember a priest holds the honor
of God on his lips? Will you not trouble yourself to spread
the fire He wishes so much enkindled? If you will not study
and prepare when young, what when you are old? This is a
mother's lesson." Her own aim in education was indeed to
"spread the fire" of God's love. But Mother Seton did not
find the religious life easy, especially when it involved exercising authority. She wrote, "I pray, meditate, speak, and
direct the community, and that with regularity, resignation,
and simplicity of heart. However, it is not I, but a species of
machine, pleasing doubtless to the compassionate Father; but
a being altogether different from the one in which the soul
acts." Mother Seton was by nature high-spirited. "Ardent
and independent" were her own words about herself, and
for years she had to struggle with spiritual desolation, "a dry
and barren tree." In the same letter she continued:

> In meditation, prayer, communion, I find no soul. In the
> beings who surround me I, who love them so tenderly—I find
> no soul. In the tabernacle, where I know that He is, I do not
> see Him, I do not feel His presence. A thousand deaths might be
> suspended over my head in order to force me to deny, and I

would brave them all rather than hesitate even for a single instant; yet it seems to me that He is not there for me.

And again, elsewhere:

> Every day I ask myself what I do for God in the modest lot that has fallen to me; and I see that I do nothing, only smile, give caresses, exercise patience, write, pray, and live, in the expectation of the Lord. O my dear Lord, let thy reign begin.

God had reigned in Mother Seton's heart all her life; but longing for His glory in Heaven was increasingly strong. She was very fond of that lovely hymn "Jerusalem, my happy home," for which she composed the music of a tune.[3] The call to the Heavenly Jerusalem came at last on January 4, 1821, when she died at the Emmitsburg convent at the age of only forty-seven. Among her last words to her community were, "Be children of the Church." Sixty years later the first steps toward Mother Seton's beatification were taken at the instance of Cardinal Gibbons; she is the first American of English descent to be a candidate for canonization.

Like, among others, the two Marys of the Incarnation (Acarie and Martin), Mother Seton entered on the path of holiness while living "in the world," a wife and a mother of children; and a word must be said about those children to whom she was so deeply devoted all her days: when there was question of a conflict between her duties to them and to her community, she declared, "My dear children have the first right, which must ever remain inviolable." The eldest, Anna, died before her mother, as a member of her young com-

---

[3] This gave rise to the astonishing mistake that Mother Seton had also written the words. They were in fact written in England about 200 years before she was born.

munity; Catherine also became a nun, but lived to the age
of ninety; Rebecca, crippled in an accident, died young, and
Richard, too, died unmarried; William, a naval officer, alone
had children to carry on the name. One of his sons was Archbishop Robert Seton; another, also William, was a lawyer,
soldier, and scholar, and a worthy representative of his
holy grandmother.

15

PATRONESS OF IMMIGRANTS

❦

IT IS with St. Frances Cabrini as with the Martyrs of
North America—she is now so well known that no more
need be said here than briefly to sketch that great career that
began in Italy, ended so far as this world is concerned in Chicago, and was consummated when she was canonized in St.
Peter's basilica in Rome on July 7, 1946.

Her father was a well-to-do farmer in Lombardy, where
Frances was born in 1850, the youngest of thirteen children.
She was trained to be a schoolteacher; but when she was
twenty-two she sought admittance first to one convent, then
to another, only to be refused by both on the ground of poor
health. The priest of Codogno, however, had a small orphanage in his parish and this was being badly mismanaged by its
eccentric foundress, Antonia Tondini; so Don Serrati asked
Frances to help in it and try to turn its staff into a religious
community. With a good deal of hesitation she agreed to take
it on.

Thus Frances entered upon what an English Benedictine
nun has called "a novitiate of sorts, compared to which one in
a regular convent would have been child's play." Antonia
Tondini had consented to her coming, but put every difficulty
in her way. Frances stuck to it, however, obtained several

recruits, and with seven of them took her first vows in 1877.
At the same time the bishop of Lodi put her in charge. This
aggravated Sister Tondini's opposition to fantastic lengths,
and although Sister Cabrini persevered patiently, the bishop
decided after another three years that the orphanage must
be closed. He sent for Frances and said to her, "You want to
be a missionary sister. Now is the time. I don't know any insti-
tute of missionary sisters; so found one yourself." And quite
simply she went out to do it. With her seven faithful followers she moved into a disused friary, where she drew up a rule
for the community. Its work was to be principally the education of girls in any land, and its name The Missionary Sisters
of the Sacred Heart. The constitutions were approved by the
bishop of Lodi, and within a few years two more houses were
opened.

The above few particulars are easily written; the actuality
was anything but easy. But Mother Cabrini overcame all difficulties and tiresome obstructions, and in 1887 she went to
seek the Holy See's approbation of her little congregation and
permission to open a house in Rome. People of experience
tried to dissuade her, pointing out that seven years' trial was
far too little. But Mother Cabrini made an impression.
Approval was given to her enterprise, and she was asked to
open not one but two houses in Rome, a free school and a children's home.

From early years Frances had been attracted by the idea
of work in China, but now people were trying to make her
look the other way. At that time the religious and social con-
dition of Italian immigrants in America was causing deep dis-
quiet; and Msgr. Scalabrini, Bishop of Piacenza, who had

established the Society of St. Charles to work among them, suggested that some of Mother Cabrini's congregation go out there to help these priests in their mission. She would not consider the proposal. Then the archbishop of New York, Msgr. Corrigan, sent her a formal invitation. She was worried; almost everyone was pointing in the same direction. Then she had a very impressive dream, and she determined to consult the pope himself. And Leo XIII said, "Not to the East, but to the West."

As a child Frances Cabrini had once fallen into a river, and ever after she had a fear of water. Now, with six of her sisters, she set out on the first of many voyages across the Atlantic; and on March 31, 1889, they landed in New York. Their first experiences on arrival were not very encouraging. They had been asked to organize an orphanage for Italian children and to take charge of a school, but, though warmly welcomed, they found no home ready for them, and they had to spend the first night at least in lodgings that were filthy and verminous. And when Mother Cabrini met Archbishop Corrigan she learned that, because of disagreements between himself and the benefactress concerned, the orphanage scheme had fallen through, and the school consisted of pupils but no habitable building. The archbishop wound up by telling her that he could see nothing for it but that the sisters should go back to Italy. To which St. Frances replied with characteristic firmness and decision, "No, Monsignor, not that. The pope sent me here, and here I must stay."

The archbishop was impressed by this straightforward little woman from Lombardy, and also by her credentials from Rome; so he let them stay and arranged for their temporary accommodation. Within a few weeks St. Frances had made friends with the benefactress, Countess Cesnola, reconciled her with Archbishop Corrigan, found a house for her community, and made a start with the orphanage. In three months she was able to revisit Italy, taking with her the first two Italo-American recruits to her congregation.

When she returned to America it was to take over West Park, on the Hudson, from the Society of Jesus. The growing orphanage was transferred to this house, which also became the mother house and novitiate for the Missionary Sisters in the United States. Soon Mother Cabrini had to make a trying journey to Managua in Nicaragua where, in difficult and sometimes dangerous conditions, she took over an orphanage and opened a boarding school. On her way back she visited New Orleans at the request of its archbishop, the revered Francis Janssens. Here the Italians were in an especially sad state: they included some wild, lawless elements, and only a short while before, eleven of them had been lynched by infuriated but no less lawless Americans. The upshot of the visit was that St. Frances was able to make a foundation in New Orleans.

Everybody knows that Frances Cabrini was an extraordinarily able woman: her works speak for her. Like Blessed Philippine Duchesne, she was slow in learning English and never lost her strong accent; but this, apparently, was no handicap in successful dealings with people of all kinds, and those with whom she had financial business (necessarily many and important) were particularly impressed. In only one direction did her tact fail, and that was in relation to non-Catholic Christians. She met such in America for the first time

in her life, and it took her a long time to recognize their good
faith and to appreciate their good lives. Her rather shocking
remarks about them in earlier days sprang from ignorance
and consequent lack of understanding. But she was farseeing
and ready to learn, and did not reject things simply because
they were new, as her ideas about children's education show.
And St. Frances was a born ruler, as strict as she was just.
Sometimes she seems to have been a little too strict, and not
to have seen where her inflexibility was leading. It is not
clear, for instance, how she thought she was upholding sexual
morality when she refused to take illegitimate children in her
fee-paying schools: it would appear to be a gesture that penal-
ized only the innocent. But the greatest saints are not immune
from errors of judgment; love ruled all, and her strictness
was no deterrent to the affection she gave and received.

The year 1892, fourth centenary of the discovery of the
New World, was also marked by the birth, in somewhat difficult circumstances, of one of the best known of Mother
Cabrini's undertakings, the Columbus Hospital in New York.
Then, after a visit to Italy, she had to go to Costa Rica, Panama, Chile, across the Andes into Brazil, and so to Buenos
Aires, where she opened a high school for girls; and of those
who pointed out the difficulties and hazards of what she was
doing, she inquired, "Are we doing this—or is our Lord?"
Then to Italy again (where she had a lawsuit and other
troubles on hand), to France, and to England. And so it
went on for another dozen years. If travelers want a more
recent and less shadowy patron saint than St. Christopher, it
should surely be St. Frances Cabrini: her love for all the
children of God took her back and forth over the globe from

Rio to Rome, from Southwark to Seattle. Those journeys
would be no light undertaking today: fifty years ago they
would have been an ordeal and strain for the strongest of men
and the hardiest of travelers. One of the things that light-
ened them for Mother Cabrini was her love of natural scen-
ery.

By the time the Missionary Sisters received their final
approbation from the Holy See in 1907, the eight members
of 1880 had increased to more than a thousand in eight
countries; St. Frances had made more than fifty foundations,
responsible for free schools and high schools and hospitals
and other establishments, and no longer working in America
for Italian immigrants alone. The trials and troubles attend-
ant on these foundations, including the opposition of factions
and individuals, were heavy, and from 1911 Mother Cabrini's
health was failing: she was then sixty-one and physically
worn out. But it was not until six years later that she was seen
to be failing alarmingly, and then the end came with extreme
suddenness. No one was present when St. Frances Xavier
Cabrini died in the convent at Chicago on December 22, 1917.

Though she is particularly honored as the first citizen of
the United States to be canonized, her glory belongs to Italy
as well as to America, to the Church and to mankind. Her
spirit lives on in her congregation, those Missionary Sisters
whom she urged to "Love one another. Sacrifice yourselves
for your sisters readily and always. Be kind to them, never
sharp, never harsh. Don't nurse resentment: be meek and
peaceable."

16

PIONEER PRIEST

❧

AMONG those heroic missionaries who spent their lives laying the foundations of the Church in the West a century ago is an Italian who we may hope will one day be beatified and canonized. Samuel Charles Gaetano Mazzuchelli, a friar of St. Dominic's Order of Preachers, was born at Milan in Italy in 1806, into a well-known family of that city, and in due course was professed a Dominican. "In religion" he took the name of Augustine, but he seems always to have been known in America by his first baptismal name—or indeed sometimes as "Father Kelly." The turning point of his life came when he was twenty-two and about to be ordained subdeacon at Rome. Father Frederick Rese, vicar general to the first bishop of Cincinnati, Edward Fenwick (himself a Dominican), was in the city asking for missionaries, and within a few months Mazzuchelli found himself being welcomed by Bishop Fenwick on the banks of the Ohio. In 1830 he was ordained priest and sent to minister among the French and Indians of the island of Mackinac between Lake Michigan and Lake Huron. His "parish" stretched to the Mississippi. But that was nothing—the diocese of Cincinnati covered all Ohio, Michigan, and Wisconsin.

Writing for American readers there is no need to describe

the conditions in which the missionary clergy of those days lived and worked; moreover, space is limited, and for that reason neither can the heroic labors of Father Mazzuchelli be detailed. I have before me a book dealing with only the first half of his priestly life, and that alone covers more than 300 pages. It must, then, be enough to say that from 1830 until 1835 he ministered at Mackinac, Arbre Croche, Sault Saint Marie, Point-Saint-Ignace, Green Bay, Kaukauna, Portage, and Prairie du Chien, during which time he baptized 1,500 children and drew up a prayer book in the Winnebago language printed at Detroit in 1833. In the next twenty years he built the first churches and formed the nucleus for parishes and dioceses at Galena, Dubuque,[1] Davenport, and a score of other places in Illinois, Iowa, and Wisconsin. Not until 1839 did he have a brother priest within a hundred miles.

An interesting incident in the early days at Mackinac was when Father Mazzuchelli revived in an informal way the public penance of the early Church. (Perhaps he did so on other occasions—I do not know.) A certain man by his misbehavior had given public scandal, which brought a reflected disgrace on all the Catholics of the locality. When he had expressed his repentance, Father Mazzuchelli declared that so public a scandal required a no less public penance. It was January, and the man was told that until the following Easter he would be allowed to assist at Mass only from the steps of the church, cut off from the rest of the congregation. He accepted this penance, and carried it out so submissively that on the first Sunday in Lent Father Mazzuchelli dispensed

---

[1] His St. Raphael's in Dubuque was the first Catholic church in Upper Louisiana Territory and became the cathedral of the first diocese in that territory.

him from the remainder and publicly readmitted him among the rest of the faithful.

Another notable practice in view of present-day discussions was when he undertook the evangelization of the Menominee Indians at Green Bay, Wisconsin, where he built the first church and school. At Vespers (yes, Vespers) on Sundays and holy days alternate verses of the psalms, hymn, and *Magnificat* were sung in their own language by the Indian congregation; this, Father Mazzuchelli assures us, kindled a strong devotion in them: "they felt a great happiness at being able to sing the Lord's praises in His own house."

It is sometimes made a matter of reproof against otherwise good Catholics that so many of them seem indifferent to the harm that can be done by hard liquor, and are inclined to laugh, perhaps even to sneer, at teetotallers. Like so many other missionaries before and after him, Father Samuel experienced that one of the worst enemies of his work was strong drink, whether among the whites or the Indians. And it is interesting to find that this Italian, to whom wine was an even more natural drink than water, became a strong upholder of the Catholic Total Abstinence Society, whose members made a solemn promise before a priest "to abstain from any intoxicating drink, unless used medicinally and by order of a physician." When that society had become established among his people, Father Mazzuchelli wrote, "Piety actually made visible progress from day to day, in proportion as the virtue of temperance won its blessed victories."

After thirteen years as a simple missionary Father Samuel extended his activities to the supply of those things that his own work had helped to make necessary—schools and teach-

ers, a regular supply of clergy trained to carry on what he
and his fellows had set going. At Sinsinawa Mound in Wisconsin he founded a college for boys; he established a new
province of his order which, though very soon merged in an
older province, is now perpetuated by the province of Saint
Albert the Great; he founded the first school for girls in Wisconsin, St. Clara's Academy, and superintended it for twelve
years; and he founded and directed the congregation of
teaching sisters now so well known as the Sinsinawa Dominicans.

That all this was not done without sufferings and trials,
setbacks, disappointments, discouragements—and those sometimes from quarters whence they would not be expected—is
a matter that need not be labored. When young Samuel
Mazzuchelli went out into the wilderness of what was then
the Northwest he was no rough pioneering type: he was a
refined and cultured European, well read, fond of music and
art, something of an architect and sculptor. He put the whole
of himself and his talents at the disposal of the people whom
he had come to serve, in matters secular no less than in those
religious. He designed the first courthouse at Galena, Illinois,
and Fort Madison, Iowa, and collaborated on the first capitol
at Iowa City (with a lovely winding staircase). It is known
that he planned the town of Shullsburg, Wisconsin, and gave
the names of the virtues to its streets. Persistent tradition also
has it that he inspired the city-plans of Davenport and Iowa
City, Iowa. He was chaplain to the Wisconsin territorial
assembly; he wrote in the pioneer press and took part in public debates; and when the crash came he took his stand against
Negro slavery. Of the lighter events of his life, perhaps none

could have given more amusement to the onlooker than his interview with the Mormon leader, Joseph Smith. "I'm always glad to meet a Catholic priest," said the prophet. "You fellows mind your own business and take care of your people. . . ."

It was almost inevitable that some people should want to make Mazzuchelli a bishop, but he gave them no encouragement. "To live retired and unknown to the world is a great happiness," he wrote to Bishop Loras of Dubuque in 1850. "If the Lord is not very much displeased with me, He will permit me to work in oblivion before the world and enable me to know Him more and more. Amen."

On the night of February 15, 1864, during a severe small-pox plague, Father Samuel was summoned by a sick call. In his hurry he took neither cloak nor coat, and rode through bitter weather from Benton, Wisconsin, to New Diggings. He went down with pneumonia. On February 23, surrounded by the sisters of the community he had founded, but before the nearest priest could get there, he fell asleep in the Lord. He was fifty-seven years old.

That Father Samuel was a very holy man as well as a great missionary can perhaps best be realized in reading between the lines of his *Memoirs of a Missionary Apostolic*, published in Milan in 1844 and translated by Sister Mary Benedicta, of the Sinsinawa Dominicans, in 1915. There has even been a full-length book about him in French (by Sister Rosemary Crepeau, of Rosary College, River Forest); and in 1950 Mary Ellen Evans produced a most readable account of his career called *The Seed and the Glory*. It must be agreed with Serge Barrault that "Mazzuchelli is one of the great figures in the apostolate carried on by European priests in the younger days of the United States."

It is perhaps not unfitting that this book be brought to an end with the final words of Francis Palou to the prologue of his Life of Father Junípero Serra, words which I venture to make my own:

> I do not forget that neither Homer among the poets, Demosthenes among the orators, nor yet Aristotle or Solon among the wise, were free from error; for though they were eminently great as poets, orators, and philosophers, yet were they still men. The limitations of our nature are ever humiliating. And as long as men write there will always be others on the lookout for their mistakes. Please bear in mind thine own weakness and have compassion upon mine. Farewell.